Soundings

CW01424467

Issue 30

Living Well

FOUNDING EDITORS
Stuart Hall
Doreen Massey
Michael Rustin

EDITOR
Jonathan Rutherford

MANAGING EDITOR
Sally Davison

ASSOCIATE EDITORS
Geoff Andrews
Sarah Benton

REVIEWS EDITOR
Jo Littler

ART EDITOR
Tim Davison

EDITORIAL OFFICE
Lawrence & Wishart
99a Wallis Road
London E9 5LN

ADVERTISEMENTS
Write for information to
Soundings,
c/o Lawrence & Wishart

SUBSCRIPTIONS
2005 subscription rates are (for three issues):
UK: Institutions £75, Individuals £35
Rest of the world: Institutions £85, Individuals £45

ISSN 1362 6620
ISBN 1-905007-22-1

Printed in Great Britain by
Cambridge University Press, Cambridge

Soundings is published three times a year, in
autumn, spring and summer by:
Lawrence & Wishart,
99a Wallis Road, London E9 5LN.
Email: soundings@lwbks.co.uk

Website: www.lwbooks.co.uk/journals/soundings/contents.html

CONTENTS

———————————————— Continued on next page ————————————————

Continued from previous page

NOTES ON CONTRIBUTORS

Moniza Alvi's latest book is *Souls*, Bloodaxe 2005.

Caroline Bassett teaches and researches digital media in the Department of Media and Film at the University of Sussex.

Farhad Dalal is a member of the South Devon Psychotherapy and Counselling Service. He works as an organisational consultant, psychotherapist and group analyst. His publications include *Taking the Group Seriously* (Jessica Kingsley 1998) and *Race, Colour and the Processes of Racialization: New Perspectives from Group Analysis, Psychoanalysis and Sociology* (Brunner-Routledge 2002).

Eunice de Souza retired as head of the English Department of St Xavier's College Bombay about five years ago. She has published four books of poetry (one with Polygon in Edinburgh), two novellas, and has edited various volumes for Oxford University Press India. Her poems have been translated into Portuguese, Finnish and Italian.

John Gittings first visited China in 1971, and was *The Guardian*'s China specialist and foreign leader-writer for many years. His latest book, *The Changing Face of China: From Mao to Market*, is published by OUP in July 2005.

Stephan Harrison is a geomorphologist working in the School of Geography and the Environment at Oxford University. He has worked in the mountains of central Asia, Patagonia, central Europe and northern Scandinavia on climate change issues.

Stephen Maddison is Senior Lecturer in Cultural Studies, University of East London, and the author of *Fags, Hags and Queer Sisters*, published by Macmillan.

Jacqueline Rose is Professor of English at Queen Mary, University of London. She is author of *The Question of Zion*, Princeton University Press 2005.

Michael Rustin is a founding editor of *Soundings*.

Molly Scott Cato is the Green Party's economics speaker. Her research focuses on community economic development and she is author of a book on regeneration of the South Wales Valleys, *The Pit and the Pendulum: A Cooperative Future for Work in the Welsh Valleys in 2004*; and of *Market, Schmarket*.

Hetan Shah is Programme Director at the new economics foundation. He is co-author of *A Well-being Manifesto*, which can be downloaded from www.neweconomics.org.

Tom Shakespeare has researched and taught sociology at the Universities of Cambridge, Sunderland, Leeds and Newcastle. He has written and broadcast widely on disability, genetics and bioethics. His co-authored books include *The Sexual Politics of Disability* (1996) and *Genetic Politics* (2002). His new book, *Disability Rights and Wrongs*, is due from Routledge in 2006.

George Szirtes was born in Budapest in 1948 and came to England as a refugee in 1956. His most recent book, *Reel* (Bloodaxe 2004) was the winner of the T.S. Eliot Prize.

Sarah Wardle is poet-in-residence with Tottenham Hotspur FC. Her latest book, *Score!* is published by Bloodaxe 2005.

Andrea Westall is Deputy Director of the new economics foundation.

Fiona Williams is Professor of Social Policy and Director of the CAVA Research Centre for the Study of Politics, Practices and Ethics of Care at the University of Leeds: www.leeds.ac.uk/cava.

Ken Worpole has been associated with New Left and community politics since the 1960s. He now works as a policy adviser and writer on twentieth century urban design and landscape. His most recent book is *Last Landscapes: the architecture of the cemetery in the West* (Reaktion Books 2003). He is married to the photographer, Larraine Worpole. Website: www.worpole.net.

Yang Lian's work was banned in China in 1983, and he has lived in exile since 1989, when he organised memorial services for the dead of Tiananmen while in New Zealand. He lives in London. His books include, *Where the Sea Stands Still: New Poems* (translated by Brian Holton), Bloodaxe 1999.

Nira Yuval-Davis is a Professor and Graduate Course Director in Gender, Sexualities and Ethnic Studies at the University of East London. Her publications include *Gender and Nation* (Sage 1997); *Women, Citizenship and Difference* (Zed 1999); *Warning Signs of Fundamentalisms* (WLUML 2004). She is currently working a monograph on *Securing Gendered Belonging/s: Human Security, Human Rights and Contemporary Politics of Belonging.*

Living well

In this issue of *Soundings*, almost all the contributors write about the ways we live our lives. Many of the anxieties and problems of twenty-first century life in the post-industrial part of the world remain unaddressed by mainstream and traditional left politics - for example problems such as mental illness, insecurity, over-work, social marginalisation. When New Labour does try to address such issues, they often resort to the idiom of discipline, whether this takes the form of a banal endorsement of banning hoodies from public spaces, or the authoritarian impulse behind the imposition of identity cards. Contributors in this issue try to find alternative ways of grappling with some of these questions.

There are two main sets of arguments here. The first set can be characterised as arguments aimed at displacing narrow neo-liberal concerns from the central place they hold in decision-making about all areas of life. Thus Fiona Williams argues that we should place the concept of care at the centre of political decision-making. She explores the political implications of displacing the dominating themes of work and consumption from their central position in the 'hard-working families' agenda. Hetan Shah outlines the political implications of a well-being approach, and suggests some ways in which it might link to a left agenda. He makes the important point that what we decide to measure as a mark of progress in society will itself be a major determinant of policy. Andrea Westall develops this point in her exploration of alternative resources for economics, arguing that we need to move away from the limited agendas of traditional economics. Molly Scott Cato writes from a green economic perspective, arguing that we should focus our attention on the question of control over our jobs and our working lives - including our household and caring work.

This first set of arguments continues the exploration of alternative economic philosophies and policies that was begun in *Soundings* 29 with Edward Fulbrook's article on post autistic economics. We will continue this theme in the next issue, with articles by David Purdy on post materialism and left political economy, and James Robertson on money.

The second set of articles continues the discussion on identity from *Soundings* 29. Identity politics addresses questions about how we define ourselves (and in many cases how we resist the definition of others); its emergence on to (parts of) the left agenda through the identity movements and cultural analysis of the 1970s and 1980s helped to extend critical political thought to embrace a much wider agenda than hitherto. These wider forms of politics are a crucial resource for resisting the narrow focus of neo-liberalism - which is restricted both in its political aims, and in the impoverished view it takes of the individual.

Farhad Dalal, arguing from a perspective informed by group analysis, looks at the often invisible ways through which people in institutions perpetuate racial inequality; he shows how the dynamics of groups contribute to racialisation processes - and thus offers compelling evidence that an equality agenda based on individual rights will never be able to get to grips with what goes on inside institutions. Tom Shakespeare tracks some of the changes in the disability movement over the last thirty years, and argues that the old model of disability identity politics, largely based on valorising the self-identity of the disabled, could sometimes lead to the reinforcement of barriers; he argues for a 'wider, looser, more dynamic and self-critical disability community', working for inclusion and recognition in the wider society. Nira Yuval-Davis looks at problems in contemporary theories of cosmopolitanism, evoking some of the difficulties that arise from its parallels with universalism; she argues that it is important not to seek to obliterate difference, particularly from an assumed position of detachment. Her exploration of how these concerns link to debates within theories of human rights is complex and illuminating. Finally, Jacqueline Rose's article on the spirit of Zionism (extracted from her recent book) provides fascinating insights into the relationship between nations and the psyche.

Elsewhere in the issue, Ken Worpole looks at another issue that affects the quality of our lives, in looking at ways in which architecture can contribute to more humane cities. Stephan Harrison writes on climate change in Kazakhstan, offering compelling evidence of global warming, and showing the serious effects it has for many people in regions not often recognised as under threat. John Gittings provides analysis of changes currently underway in China, and Michael Rustin looks at what lies ahead for New Labour in its third term.

The next issue of *Soundings* will be the tenth anniversary issue and will look to the future. The focus will be on children and young people, with articles by Lisa Harker on childcare, Madeleine Bunting and Rowan Williams on the politics of childhood, and a roundtable discussion on girlhood. There will also be debate about the future of the left from, amongst others, Lawrence Grossberg and Martin McIvor.

SD

How we live now

Jonathan Rutherford

I was using a Barclays Bank cash machine, my card was ejected, and as I waited for the money a strap line flashed up on the screen: 'Open the door to your dreams'. My money rolled out and then it was gone, replaced by the image of an open door. It reminded me of a recent Lloyds Bank leaflet that asked: 'How can we help you live your life?' Capitalism offers us more than material goods. It promises us the good life - dreams, hope, love, a secure future. It has provided majorities in the industrialised countries with historically unprecedented levels of affluence and individual choice. In the last thirty years, Gross Domestic Product has almost doubled in the UK. But its profit-seeking activities are a colonising force which threatens the substantiality and continuity of social relations. The market reconstitutes connections between people as economic relations between individuals and things. It has created a tantalising world of commodity consumption that makes people feel lonely, dissatisfied and insecure.

Standards of living are increasingly defined by the purchasing of status giving, positional goods. Their value diminishes as more people acquire them, creating a spiralling of consumption as people strive to maintain their social standing. To fuel this dynamic and boost demand, finance capitalism has disconnected consumer desire from individual available earnings by aggressively selling consumer credit. In July 2004, consumer debt exceeded £1 trillion in Britain, of which £183.6 billion was unsecured debt on personal loans, credit and store cards.[1] In recent years, personal loans have expanded into the sub prime and home loan markets, charging exorbitant interest rates to the poor who no longer have access to welfare benefits. With its relentless pursuit of profit, capitalism is a revolutionary force without morality. As Joseph

---

1. Credit Action, 'Debt Statistics', March 2005, www.creditaction.org.uk.

Schumpeter warned us, we should fear its success as much as its failure. Capitalism's 'creative destruction', and the spiralling of status seeking consumption amongst a small minority of the global population, is shattering the ecological fabric of the earth. It is unsustainable.

What about the failure of capitalism? As manufacturing industry continues its decline and retail sales and house prices begin to fall, the affluent amongst us can be reminded of the havoc it wreaks. Between 1980 and 1999, the richest 1 per cent of the UK population increased its share of national income from around 6 per cent to 13 per cent.[2] In 2002, this 1 per cent owned approximately 25 per cent of the UK's marketable wealth. In contrast, 50 per cent of the population shared only 6 per cent of total wealth.[3] Exclude housing from these estimates, and inequality increases even further. In 2000, 50 per cent of families had £600 or less in savings, and 25 per cent were £200 or more in debt.[4] Large sections of the working class, particularly in the post industrial towns of the north, and ethnic minorities, have been condemned to generations of gruelling poverty, crime and hopelessness. And even for the relatively affluent, debt is reducing many to a state of indentured consumption and a future tied to unremitting work. However much we accumulate in the way of worldly goods, there remains a fear without an object. An anxiety about 'something which is nothing'. What is left that is durable and trustworthy?

The penetration of market relations into the social fabric of people's lives has generated a set of 'post-material' social problems - widespread mental ill health, systemic loneliness, growing numbers of psychologically damaged children, eating disorders, obesity, alcoholism, drug addiction, compulsions to shop, spend and accumulate things, the breakdown of relationships and marriages. Thus, for example, the cost of mental health problems in the UK is estimated at £93 billion a year, in lost productivity, health care spending and reductions in quality of life.[5] Stress, anxiety and depression

2. Institute of Public Policy Research, *The State of the Nation*, August 2005.
3. National Statistics, 'Share of the Wealth', www.statistics.gov.uk/cci/nugget.asp?id=2.
4. James Banks, Zoe Smith, Matt Wakefield, *The Distribution of Financial Wealth in the UK: Evidence from 2000 BHPS Data*, Institute of Fiscal Studies, WP02/21, 2002, p7, www.ifs.org.uk. See also Mike Brewer et al, *Poverty and Inequality in Britain: 2004*, Commentary 96, www.ifs.org.uk.
5. Mental Health Foundation, *Time for Public Mental Health: A briefing from the Mental Health Foundation in advance of the White Paper on Public Health*, 2004, www.mentalhealth.org.uk.

account for a third of all working days lost. A survey of 17,000 people by the charity Mind found that 20 per cent of respondents found work 'very' or 'extremely' stressful.[6] A conservative estimate of the cost to the NHS of alcohol related conditions is as much as £1.7 billion per annum.[7] 'Mental disorders' are now among the leading causes of world disease and disability. The World Health Organisation predicts that by 2020 depression will rank second behind heart disease as a 'leading cause of the global disease burden'. A survey on sleep undertaken by the Future Foundation reveals that one in four people in the UK are finding it difficult to sleep well. The biggest cause of sleep disorders is anxiety. Women coping with paid work, housework and childcare suffer more than men. The survey's project manager, Brian Garvey, in an attempt to explain the findings, said: 'Fear has become a powerful tool in society. A nervousness permeates our current lives' (*Observer*, 13.3.05).

Stress, depression, breakdown, bullying, violence might appear to have their source in dysfunctional individuals, but they are dysfunctions that belong to the wider social network. Social life is not external to inner psychological reality; its matrix of conscious and unconscious communications form the innermost being of individual personality. Shame, failure, feelings of worthlessness, hopelessness and meaninglessness are our modern dreads, and they arise in the class, family and social relations that we grow up in. After three decades of the neo-liberal economic order, we are a society that is beset by loss; loss of belonging, loss of political purchase on the world, loss of hope. We live in a paradox. We are collectively, politically inert, yet we exist in a state of continuous activity, whipped on by the exhortation to be 'hard working families'. Companies are re-engineered, institutions re-configured, departments re-organised, working practices reviewed, schools repeatedly inspected, employees monitored and appraised. Goals, visions and mission statements are invented and re-defined. Politicians urge us to join the enterprise culture, become more business-like, embrace change. But in reality, this dynamic of permanent change simply reproduces the status quo. Nothing actually, meaningfully, changes. We are living in a social recession. There is no politics to give voice to our protest. There is no alternative which offers a better future

6. Mind, *Stress and the Workplace*, 2005, www.mind.org.uk.
7. Institute of Alcohol Studies, Fact Sheet, *Alcohol and Health*, 2005, p8, www.ias.org.uk.

that is more equal, more just, more tolerant, and more kind.

Living well

The future of the democratic left depends on our being able to offer this alternative. How are we to live? The idea of 'living well' originates with Aristotle. Happiness is not defined by a transient moment, but is the good that we pursue 'in a complete life'. For the Stoic philosopher Seneca (circa.4BC-AD65), living was an art: 'But learning how to live takes a whole life, and, which may surprise you more, it takes a whole life to learn how to die'.[8] For Michel De Montaigne, writing in the sixteenth century, the act of self creation was integral to his humanity and his relationship with others; a process of coming to know himself which embraced uncertainty as the primary fact of being alive. The chief aim in life is pleasure: 'Even in virtue our ultimate aim … is pleasure'.[9] Virtue is not to be found in an external law or deity. It grows out of the pleasure we discover in being with ourselves, and with those we love and befriend. Ethics is the endeavour to go on being.

Who speaks in public of such things today? The left once cultivated this language, but it is now bereft of a vision of a better life. The concern with living well is not simply a valorisation of private individualism, but indicative of the difficulty individuals have at certain historical moments in finding meaning and purpose in life. There is a need for a politics of social transformation which takes seriously the importance of living well. We can find precursors in the traditions of ethical socialism, anarchism, the New Life, Quakerism, but these tended to reproduce an idea of the good life that was singular and too prescriptive for our plural society. John Stuart Mill provides a good example of the liberal attempt to avoid this dilemma. In *On Liberty*, he asserts that the cultivation of individuality is central to well being. Society must preserve the freedom 'of pursuing our own good in our own way'. The ultimate appeal of all ethics cannot be to an absolute morality. It must be to utility, to structure the conditions which optimise individual well being. But today the principle of utility has been discredited by the market based reforms and audit cultures in health and education. The market disables individual agency, destroys the ethic of care and service, and depoliticises the

---

8. Seneca, *Dialogues and Letters*, Penguin 1997, p66.
9. Michel De Montaigne, *The Essays: A Selection*, Penguin 1993, p18.

relationship of the individual to society. We need a new story about individual freedom and self-fulfilment that is about human interdependency and the ethic of reciprocity, not the calculative logic of the market and utility.

Stories of renewal are not conjured out of thin air; they are made on the basis of what we learn from the traditions we inherit. There are three principles we have inherited which have defined the politics of modernity: liberty, equality and fraternity. The Right laid claim to liberty, the Left made claim to equality. Each was embedded in its class and polarised as mutually exclusive to the other. Fraternity never achieved the same ideological significance as the other two principles. It was the virtue of the political activist, and the ethos of the society promised by a utopian future. But it is the tradition of fraternity which has the potential to give shape to a new narrative of individual freedom. Fraternity, in its recognition of human interdependence, is the catalyst which brings together liberty and equality. In its advocacy of the social and relational nature of human beings, the self-fulfilment of each is indivisible from the equal worth of all. We need a new ideal of fraternity - a commonwealth of difference upheld by mutual recognition.

The philosopher Paul Ricoeur (who died in May 2005) offers a way of thinking about interdependence and its relationship to the ethic of living well. In his book *Oneself as Another*, he defines an 'ethical intention' that must be central to a democratic left politics. It is: 'the desire to live well with and for others in just institutions'.[10] He examines each of the three points of this definition. The first point is 'to live well', which he describes as 'the nebulous of ideals and dreams of achievements with regard to which a life is held to be more or less fulfilled or unfulfilled' (p179). Ricoeur's second point is 'with and for others'. He describes living with and for others as 'solicitude'. Solicitude is not separate from individual self esteem; it expresses its social nature. Ricoeur explains this by using the example of friendship in which 'each loves the other as being the man he is' (p183). To be 'equal among friends' is for two friends to render to the other 'a portion equal to what he or she receives' (p184). What follows on from the giving and receiving of friendship is the idea of equality. Friendship involves the ethic of reciprocity and this sets friendship on the path to justice: 'where life together shared by a few people gives way to the distribution of shares in a plurality on

---

10. Paul Ricoeur, *Oneself as Another*, trans. Kathleen Blamey, University of Chicago Press, 1994, p180 (see also p172).

the scale of a historical, political community' (p188). Ricoeur is describing ethical life as originating in the sphere of interpersonal relationships and extending upward into the wider social realm and into the political community.

The aim of living necessitates an interdependency with others. The corollary of this interdependency is equality. Consequently, Ricoeur argues, the aim of living encompasses a sense of justice. This brings his inquiry to the third point of the 'ethical intention': 'just institutions'. Justice finds its expression in the idea of 'just institutions'. By institution Ricoeur means, 'the structure of living together as this belongs to a historical community'. The structure is irreducible to interpersonal relations and yet it is 'bound up with them in a remarkable sense' (p194). This is because institutions require political communities whose function is distributive. The distributive operations of a political community are more than the sharing implied by solicitude. Distribution involves the apportioning of 'roles, tasks, advantages and disadvantages between the members of a society' (p200). Where there is sharing there may be too much or not enough - 'the unjust man is the one who takes too much in terms of advantages or not enough in terms of burdens' (p201). Equality is the ethical core of justice. And it is not exclusive to the discourses of the political community. There is no wall between the individual and society which prevents the transition of the ethical aim from interpersonal life to the social and political realm. Equality for Ricoeur 'is to life in institutions what solicitude is to interpersonal relations' (p202). Justice holds persons to be irreplaceable and so adds to solicitude, 'to the extent that the field of application of equality is all of humanity' (p202). In an interview Ricoeur summarises his notion of ethical life as: 'the wish for personal accomplishment with and for others, through the virtue of friendship and, in relation to a third party, through the virtue of justice'.[11]

From its old incarnation as a limited and gender biased expression of solidarity, fraternity offers an ethical basis for a politics which takes seriously the idea of living well. It provides the first step in the ideological break with neo-liberalism, culturally, politically and economically. Ricoeur writes: 'This wishing to live together is silent, generally unnoticed, buried; one does not remark its existence until it falls apart' (*Critique*, p99). Putting the pieces back together is the beginning of the story.

---

11. Paul Ricoeur, *Critique and Conviction*, Polity Press, London, 1998, p60.

A THANK YOU TO CAROLE

Carole Satyamurti has been poetry editor of *Soundings* since Issue 1, which came out back in 1995. She has decided to retire from her role. We have been fortunate in having as poetry editor such a well renowned poet, who has been able to attract other poets to the pages of the journal. She has been a committed supporter of *Soundings* and a consummate editor. Talk to people about *Soundings* and they will frequently mention the poetry, because it somehow distinguishes the journal's approach to politics and culture. What is it about the poetry? Filmmaker Wim Wenders said in an interview that the best political films were those which were not about politics. It is allegory and metaphor that strike home and deliver the most powerful message. Poetry is like music. It moves us, and it brings to our minds thoughts and feelings which can transform how we view the world. The editorial group would like to thank Carole for keeping alive the poetry over the last ten years.

Jonathan Rutherford will now be taking over the editing of this section.

Carole's latest book is *Stitching The Dark: New & Selected Poems*, published by Bloodaxe Books 2005.

Duende

That great operatic bunch of tulips you bought on impulse
filled my arms with scarlet blooms already at their best,
stiff-stemmed, glossy, only a ghost of fade about them.

Days after, they were flourishing on borrowed time,
on show in satin flounces; flurry of flamenco dancers,
the increasing torsion of their scrinchy leaves,

their proudly turned heads, refusing to collapse.
It's a week now. Water in the cool yellow vase
is murky with decay, and the tulips are no longer

drawing on reserves. Past all pretence at integration,
their petals are curled rags, hurt colours.
They're entering a change of state, papery flames

writhing in silent desolation. But last week's flowers,
so bright, so upsprung, were no more essential
than these tattered queens with so much death in them.

Carole Satyamurti

A good-enough life

Developing the grounds for a political ethic of care

Fiona Williams

Fiona Williams *argues that a political ethic of care offers a new way of dealing with contemporary changes in family lives and family policies, particularly in providing a new political vocabulary that is more capable of connecting the two.*

In an article in *The Guardian* in September 2004, Martin Jacques wrote of a 'profound malaise' at the heart of Western societies:

> The very idea of what it means to be human - and the necessary conditions for human qualities to thrive - are being eroded … the intimacy on which our sense of well being rests - a product of our closest, most intimate relationships, above all in the family - is in decline … We live in an age of selfishness.

He argued that three things have occasioned this: the rise in individualism; the marketisation of all forms of human life; and the rise in communication technologies, which have contracted our private space and accelerated the pace of life. Divorce and the decline of the extended family, he suggests, have undermined family life, and the worst casualty has been the deterioration of the parent-child, especially the mother-child, relationship, because of women going out to work and couples' reluctance to make financial sacrifices.

This is a familiar argument from left and right: loss of commitment, self-seeking individualism, and children harmed by divorce or by a parenting deficit. For some it's godlessness, for others it's capitalism that has corroded community and moral character; others argue that consumerism has fostered individual acquisitiveness, infecting even the closest of our relationships. But research we have conducted over the last five years at Leeds University leads me to believe that such arguments are quite mistaken, and that they provide no basis for the changes we need in political thinking and in social and public policy.[1]

Certainly there have been changes in family lives and personal relationships. Over our lifetime many of us will cohabit, parent on our own, live alone, marry, divorce, or do all these. Our family networks may well include step-relations, close friends, same-sex partners, ex-partners, and relatives of different ethnicities. These changes are accompanied by women's greater involvement in the labour market, by children being economically dependent on their parents for longer, by the inadequacy of a single wage in a household with children, and by the growth in housing costs. We are also an ageing society with declining fertility, and a globally mobile society where families' care commitments are stretched not only across cities but across continents. But to suggest that we are witnessing the moral decline of family life is, I believe, quite mistaken. To do so too readily collapses the moral economy of capitalism into the moral agency that people exercise in their close relationships; and it underestimates the nature and extent of people's resistance and resilience as they struggle with dilemmas in their everyday caring.

Resistance and resilience

This is not to say that consumerism has not invaded the domestic sphere. One

---

1. Our research was carried out by the ESRC Research Group on *Care, Values and the Future of Welfare* (CAVA) at the University of Leeds, with funding from the Economic and Social Research Council www.leeds.ac.uk/cava (M564281001). The findings are discussed in Fiona Williams, *Rethinking Families*, Calouste Gulbenkian Foundation, 2004. The research cited here was carried out by Shelley Budgeon, Simon Duncan, Sarah Irwin, Greg Martin, Bren Neale, Sasha Roseneil, Lise Saugères, Carol Smart and Fiona Williams.

instance of this is the damage done by the food industry to the health of a generation of children. But here the problem cannot be understood though the simplistic idea that parents have simply swallowed unhealthy products and regurgitated them through take-away, throw-away relationships with each other and their children. The public support in the spring of 2005 for a campaign for state intervention to raise the nutritional standards of school dinners demonstrated the resistance of parents to the idea that they were to blame because they made wrong food 'choices', or because they don't care about their children's health; and it also exposed the consequences of the contracting out of school dinners and the deskilling of dinner ladies.

The contemporary organisation of working life places enormous strains on family life, but this does not mean that it inevitably corrupts what people seek from their relationships. Take the example of the strike in July 2003 by check-in staff at British Airways. The strike gained national media coverage for disrupting international holiday air flights, and this was amplified by the fact that the mainly women strikers were more usually known for their civility than their civil disobedience. To begin with, many reports in newspapers and interviews with trade union leaders identified the cause of the strike as dissatisfaction with changed conditions; and the women were presented by the media as both selfish (spoiling holidays) and laggards (not adapting to a new electronic clocking on system). But they did not mention the nub of the grievance: that rosters had been changed without warning and threatened to disturb the very carefully negotiated child care plans that many of the mothers had in place. These involved complex, time-managed connection points for mothers and fathers and grandmothers to exchange child care responsibilities. The women's actions chimed with one of our research findings on how mothers with young children make decisions around work and care: working mothers' investment in employment is based upon their own and their networks' moral reasoning about what is right and proper for their children. They do not act as individualist 'rational economic actors' where financial costs and benefits determine decisions. Money does matter of course to working mothers, but decisions about working are also taken in the context of being able to provide the quality of care they think is best for their children. When this moral reasoning behind the strike emerged, it changed the way trade unions, employers and the media described it: it turned into a grievance over 'work/

life balance'. Kevin Curran, the general secretary of the GMB, was quoted as saying that 'time is the new money, and work-life balance and the quality of people's lives will become a major part of the collective bargaining agenda'.

People care a great deal about doing the right thing by the people they cherish. Far from a loss of commitment, they are anxious to carry out their commitments in the ways they think fit, given the different pressures in their lives. That was one of the main findings in our in-depth interviews with almost four hundred people from different localities about the things that matter to them in their experiences of parenting and partnership. As well as looking at work and care, we focused on other areas of change - what happens to relationships with the wider family following divorce, who do people turn to when they live in 'un-familiar' ways, and how do people maintain kinship commitments when these are in different continents? We also looked at what values are important to community and self-help groups who organise around these issues, and to larger voluntary organisations. Given the degree of change, we were interested in getting a grass-roots view of the practical ethics that inform how people take decisions in their relationships of care and intimacy, rather than a top-down view of 'family values'.

We were also concerned that much of the debate on changing family lives takes place with little reference to empirical research. This is true both for the 'family-in-moral-decline' view, and for the contrasting and influential view that current changes herald a new 'individualisation' in personal life, which, it is argued, brings with it the emergence of self-actualising men and women, less bound by obligation and duty, and with greater independence to pursue more satisfying and democratic relationships. While we found some evidence for aspirations towards democratic relationships between partners, and also between children and their parents, it is also the case that change and continuity co-exist in complex ways. Many old problems persist, in spite of the context of changed opportunities for women and greater emotional investment in children; these include gender inequalities in the division of labour at home, the lack of opportunities for participation of children in institutions and decisions that affect their lives, and physical and sexual abuse of both women and children. Just as importantly, the notion of self-actualising men and women underestimates the degree to which people are deeply embedded in the relationships that matter to them, continually negotiating how to balance a sense of themselves with the needs of others around them, especially their children.

Balancing commitments

A good example of this juggling with commitments to others comes from research on how families live their lives after a divorce. These days the dominant idea is that, even if marriage is not for life, then parenting is. This was given force by the 1989 Children Act. Managing this is not always straightforward, however, especially where there has been violence, or where trust has completely broken down, or where divorce runs counter to a family's faith. In spite of this, many divorced parents, usually but not exclusively women, take it upon themselves to perform an active 'kin-keeping' role after divorce in order to sustain relationships, not just with the other parent, but with ex-grandparents and in-laws. Sometimes, of course, divorce provides the opportunity to withdraw from problematic relationships with in-laws. Either way, the ways in which people negotiate their kin-keeping tends to put a premium on what would be best for their children.

The way people re-partner after divorce also provides interesting evidence that, while the shape and texture of commitment might be changing, this does not mean that commitment itself is being abandoned; rather, people are working out different and new ways of meeting those commitments. Half of all divorced men and one third of divorced women remarry, many cohabiting en route. But some divorced parents, mothers of young children in particular, prefer to discount new relationships until their children are older, or at least to conduct them quite separately from their lives with their children. Another option some people choose is what is called a LAT relationship (living-apart-together), where partners are in committed relationships but live apart. At first sight this option might support the moral decline argument (flight from commitment; pursuing self interest) - or it might provide evidence of a single-minded search for self-actualisation. However, on looking more closely at why people opt for such an arrangement, and the financial disincentives it involves, it can be seen to be much more a question of attempting to find an equitable way of being with a new partner but at the same time sustaining your relationships with your children, or with their father or mother, or with their grandparents and your ex-in-laws. In fact, it is *all about* commitment, and balancing that with your own needs. What seemed to be important to people in sustaining these relationships through difficult changes was being able to be attentive to others' needs, adaptable to new identities, and being open to reparation.

LAT living is interesting at a more general level in revealing new constraints and mores about partnering. It is not just a feature of divorced couples' living and loving, but also of younger partners who might work in different places, or of older widowed partners who don't want to disrupt their relationships or inheritance intentions with adult children or grandchildren. The Norwegian sociologist Irene Levin says that what we might be seeing is a third major social change in the connection between sex, love and parenting. In the 1960s 'free love' - the uncoupling of sex from marriage - was the focus of moral debate. In the 1980s and 1990s it became more acknowledged that marriage and committed parenthood did not necessarily go hand in hand; and now it seems that committed sexual partnership and co-residence (and parenting) are no longer assumed. Far from being the mirror image of consumerism, this is how, over time, we are reconstituting the cultural norms of commitment in our everyday lives.

The value of friendship

Until recently friendship has been little acknowledged in the mesh of care, connection and commitment. Our research studied people who live and love without a significant or co-resident partner - those who might be regarded as highly individualised. Yet here too, while some were emotionally quite isolated, many were embedded in networks of care, commitment and support. And where they were, friends were often valued over lovers or kin for their emotional and practical significance; as one 28 year-old woman said, 'I think a friendship is for life, but I don't think a partner is - I'd marry my friends. They'd last longer'.

In his study of friendship, Ray Pahl describes how people have varied 'personal communities', in which friends as much as family can play a significant part. Also, the metaphor of friendship is commonly used to talk about the quality of relationships in families. Research on teenage children and their parents finds that both invoke friendship and companionship to describe what they value in their relationships with each other. Research on post-divorce lives suggests that qualities such as mutual respect and shared interests give more meaning to relationships that were formed through blood or law.

'Friendship' says much about what we might seek in a good relationship: confiding, sharing, fun, non-judgmental, reciprocal, if not equal. Talking recently to mothers with young children who use Sure Start services - one of the more innovative programmes introduced by New Labour in deprived areas - they told me they valued the services because the staff treated them 'like a friend'; they were not judgmental, and shared knowledge rather than handing it down. I found similar views in interviews with self-help groups for parents with particular experiences, such as having a child with drug problems, or having lost a child, or having a child with a learning disability. The mutual support they valued was based on informality, trust and non-judgmentalism.

There are important political implications here. The first is about the nature of reciprocity and solidarity in society. The political right have looked to families and family values as a way of preserving individualism and self-interest - 'looking after one's own'. The more collectively minded left have sought to maintain kin ties as the building block to social cohesion; strong kin ties are assumed to lead to strong communities, and strong communities to equal a strong and stable society. In each case, any weakening or changing of kin ties is seen as portending social disintegration. But both views fail to grasp that connectedness operates in more various ways than simply through conjugality, sexual intimacy and blood, and that the affective boundaries of reciprocity are fluid and are not fixed by kinship alone. The solidaristic base of society lies less in 'the family' and more in the practices of care and support that go on inside *and outside* of families. These constitute an important moral sentience - one that receives scant political recognition, for it is usually only as workers and consumers that politicians attempt to appeal to voters.

A second implication of the research is that when people look to give and receive support from others, they want it to involve mutual respect, trust and non-judgmentalism. I shall come back later in the article to what this might mean for political thinking, and how we organise care and support in society. But first, how have New Labour framed their policies around family lives and personal relationships?

New Labour's policies

There have been three main themes in New Labour's policies affecting family lives and personal relationships: support for 'hardworking families'; investment in children, especially through education; and emphasising parental responsibilities. In many ways, this has been the first time that Britain has had an explicit family policy, with the recognition that child care for working parents is a public and not simply an individual responsibility. The government's policies have included a commitment to abolish child poverty by 2020; a National Childcare Strategy guaranteeing a nursery place for every three or four year old; a National Carers' Strategy; the development of Sure Start to support families with young children in deprived areas; a range of tax credits to help working families on low incomes and for working parents to pay for child care; extended maternity leave and pay and paid paternity leave; and the right for parents to work part-time and to take unpaid time off to care for children. At the liberal end of their policy spectrum, New Labour has promoted measures to equalise legal and social conditions for lesbians and gay men; at the disciplinary end, they have introduced the enforcement of parental obligations in relation to children's behaviour. A new normative family is emerging, which appears, in some respects but not all, to leave the male breadwinner society behind. It revolves around the adult couple whose relationship is based on their parenting responsibilities, and whose priorities are rooted in work, economic self-sufficiency, education and good behaviour.

'Hardworking parents'

These policies are unprecedented, and they are not without tensions. The political principles which underpin this set of measures owe more to a commitment to reinforce the moral and economic imperative of the work ethic than to notions of gender equality. Paid work is said to make good parents, encourage self sufficient families, and enable men and women to make provision for themselves in the housing and pensions markets; and it makes for a competitive economy. Children's educational opportunities are less about children as participating citizens-of-the-present and more about them as worker-citizens of the future. Child care provision is the necessary corollary that enables mothers to work. The tax credit system which allows financial support for parents, also encourages the provision of child care through low-waged care in the private sector; and this kind of provision is often not affordable for low income families (unless they have access to Sure Start), as well as being less open to quality control. (The Daycare Trust found that private nurseries were less likely to institute anti-racist policies and that minority ethnic parents were less likely to use them). In addition, the policy slogan to 'make work pay' misses the point when it comes to the dilemmas that parents - and mothers especially - face in taking up paid work. These dilemmas have more to do with concerns about the affective quality of care for their children than with cost-benefit analyses. In Britain, public trust in good quality nursery care has yet to be established - many mothers prefer informal one-to-one care for their very young children to nursery care. In such a situation a focus on the moral and economic benefits of paid work is unlikely to improve matters. Furthermore, although the new 'adult worker' model is replacing the male breadwinner model, male working practices and long working hours still characterise many industries, limiting opportunities for improving mothers' opportunities either in the home or at work.

Children: citizens of the present or the future?

Tensions exist too in the focus on children. Margaret Hodge, the first ever Minister of State for Children, Young People and Families, stated that: 'we shall put children at the heart of everything we do', and this was reflected in the publication of the Green Paper *Every Child Matters* in 2003, which put forward far more universal and child-centred policies than had hitherto been proposed. The Green Paper sets out structures of accountability to protect children, to recognise their needs, and to create educational opportunities to enable them to become productive future citizens. Yet its key outcomes are more about becoming an adult than fostering the active enjoyment and negotiation of childhood. The focus on education sees children's educability as the pre-cursor to work, self-sufficiency and independence.

The 'responsibilisation' agenda

The child focus of policies has emphasised protection, yet at the same time there has been little success in reducing Britain's ranking as the most punitive country in Europe as far as children are concerned. New Labour was unresponsive to pressure to increase the age of criminal responsibility from 10 to 12; to condemn the use of custodial sentences for 12-14 year olds; and to abandon the right of parents to use 'reasonable chastisement' on their children. And they have introduced measures whereby parents can be fined and imprisoned for having a truanting child, which has helped to fuel the national anxiety about children's behaviour and 'parenting skills'. Behind much of the 'responsibilisation' discourse lies a deficit model of family life and parenting capacity. Yet amongst the parents we interviewed, it was not punishment or being told what to do that they valued; they wanted the right sort of support to carry out their parenting responsibilities.

The compassionate realism of 'good-enough' care

How do we cut through these pressures and tensions - between work and care, between investing in, protecting and punishing children, and between regulating and supporting parents? The answer lies, I believe, in developing a politics that gives value to the meaning and practices of care, love and support in people's lives. Overall we found in our research that moral reasoning based on *care* informed the way people attempted to balance their own sense of self and the needs of others. What it means to be a good mother, father, grandparent, partner, ex-partner, lover, son, daughter or friend is crucial to the way people negotiate the proper thing to do. These meanings are shaped by identities and resources wrought through class, gender, ethnicity, local practices and social networks. Of course this does not mean everyone behaves well or is successful in negotiating these things; nevertheless we found that in working through their dilemmas, certain practical ethics emerge for adults and children: an ethics that enables resilience and facilitates commitment, and lies at the heart of people's interdependency. Such an ethic includes notions of fairness, attentiveness to the needs of others, mutual respect, trust, reparation, being non-judgmental, adapting to new identities, being prepared to be accommodating, and being open to communication. These constitute the compassionate realism of 'good-enough' care.

To put this in a broader context: when we interviewed senior representatives from 24 national voluntary organisations who campaign and advise on parenting and partnering issues, the majority looked to an ethos of welfare which emphasises holistic, accessible, affordable and user-centred support for parents and children; and they advocated forms of support which place value on care as an activity, on interdependence, and on state support for financial adequacy. Such an ethos is underpinned by notions of social justice - a justice based on the promotion of anti-discriminatory policies, recognition and respect for diversity, and resistance to widening inequalities. In this these representatives placed special emphasis on valuing care and respecting childhood.

What is lacking in the current policy debate is a recognition of these ethical approaches, and of their importance in people's lives. The emphasis on work overshadows care; interdependency is the poor relation of economic self-sufficiency; and educational achievement frames child-centredness. New thinking from different quarters points to the limits of such an approach. For example, Karl Sigmund's work on the necessity of reciprocity, and recent research on happiness from Richard Layard and from Paul Martin, combine economics, psychology and philosophy to argue that connectedness and the quality of personal relationships lie at the heart of social well-being. Layard proposes that we need a 'clear concept of a common good that we can all accept and work for', and that this has to be based on what people themselves feel.[2] Happiness constitutes such a policy goal, and one whose understanding and measurement is as important - if not more so - than that of GNP. Our research on family lives leads me to a very similar conclusion, although I find Layard's proposals around family life to be too uniform to fit with the diversity of living that now exists, and the understandings of it that we have from in-depth qualitative research. He assumes, for example, that marriage is a pre-requisite for good child-rearing, and that divorce and single parenthood are intrinsically problematic. Rather than happiness, my focus is on the ethics of care.[3] My argument is that, though these practical ethics of fairness, attentiveness and so on cannot simply be transposed into the political arena, we can use them to develop a wider political ethic of care.

Developing a political ethic of care

Many recent welfare reforms - and election campaigns - have had as their basis an ethic of paid work, and the identity of consumer; but these notions are not broad enough to meet the aspirations which people have around time and the quality of their relationships. We need a political principle about care that is

---

2. Richard Layard, *Happiness: Lessons from a New Science*, Allen Lane 2005, p108.
3. See especially Joan Tronto, *Moral Boundaries: A Political Argument for an Ethic of Care*, Routledge 1993; and Selma Sevenhuijsen, *Citizenship and the Ethic of Care: Feminist Considerations on Justice, Morality and Politics*, Routledge 1998.

equivalent to the principle of paid work; and an understanding of reciprocity and interdependence which poses an alternative to individual consumption. I would suggest that care is as central to a notion of citizenship as paid work. Where the work ethic elevates the notion of independence and economic self-sufficiency, an ethic of care demands that *interdependence* be seen as the basis of human interaction. This does not deny the importance of autonomy: autonomy and independence are about the capacity for self-determination rather than simply an expectation of individual self-sufficiency.

A second point is that caring for yourself and for others is a meaningful activity in its own right. It is also a *universal* activity, and involves us all - men and women, old and young: we are all, at some level, the givers and receivers of care from others, it is an activity that binds us all. Thus, in particular, care is not an activity that is exclusive to women. But only through the public validation of care as a social good will it come to be perceived as an alternative to the breadwinner model for men and boys.

Thirdly, care contributes to social solidarity. Of course relationships can be unequal and oppressive, but in providing and receiving care and support in conditions of mutual respect, we learn and enact a practical ethics of care: attentiveness, responsibility, trust; being adaptable and accommodating to others' differences; tolerance for our own and others' human frailty; and ways of sustaining and repairing relationships. These are not just personal qualities, they are civic virtues, and therefore a part of what it means to be a citizen. In other words, care is part of citizenship.

The idea that care is a *universal* need and activity is important, because it places those with particular needs for care and support - because they are very young or disabled or frail - on a universal spectrum of needs, rather than setting them apart because of their dependency. It also recognises that those who are 'cared for' have the capacity for agency. In this way care is not just about the activity of caring for others but also about being able to care for the self. It is also about asking what support we need to 'care for the world'. By this I mean both the world outside our door - the world immediately beyond family and work - and the wider world; the politics of care implies recognition of global interdependence and inequality in issues such as migration and the environment. The political and policy questions that flow from this approach concern the *recognition* and valuing of care activities and their *redistribution* -

how should care be shared between the state, market, local communities and families, but also between individuals within (and without) families? And, in the light of migrant workers' role in providing care work, how is it shared globally? And what is 'good-enough' care?

A social environment of care

In practical terms, this approach implies that, instead of starting from the perspective of fitting care around work, policy-makers need to think much more along the lines of the parents we interviewed: how do we fit work around our care needs? We could apply the care ethic to three areas to begin with: creating time to care; creating time to be cared for; and financial and practical support for caring activities. Addressing the issue of time would involve, for example, work-related provisions of flexible hours; shorter full-time hours; paid maternity/paternity/carer leave; job-sharing; annualised hours; unpaid sabbaticals. Financial support for the costs of children could involve help to buy in care, or an allowance to cover loss of carer's wage, and would need to be tied up with anti-poverty measures such as a guaranteed minimum income and a decent state pension. There is nothing unusual in proposing these measures, but applying an ethic of care might take us further along these roads. For example, since our goals encompass social justice *and* giving care a public value, we might consider (as a number of Nordic countries have done) that there should be an element of compulsion to paternity leave. This would ensure both that

> 'instead of starting from the perspective of fitting care round work, we need to think along the lines of fitting work around our care needs'

caring becomes shared, and that employers recognise the entitlement of fathers to engage in caring activities. A care-ethic political approach could lead us to review the whole framework of the social security system: the distinction between being in work and out of work could become less fixed; and activities such as caring or volunteering could be recognised as contributions to society which require support. However, any moves in this direction would also have to ensure that caring does not become ghettoised as the paid activity of women who cannot compete elsewhere in the labour market.

Support for caring activities could involve a number of publicly provided services and forms of practical support: work-based and community based childcare services, breakfast clubs, holiday clubs; home care services, cleaning, laundry, food services, domiciliary and residential services, and advice centres. These would need to be underpinned by principles of accessibility, affordability, variety, choice, quality, flexibility, respect and user involvement. However, such forms of provision require a more fundamental shift towards a social environment of care. They need to be based on the principles of removing disabling barriers (following the example of the disability movement) to the fulfilment of the needs of those who require particular caring support, such as children or older frail people, and their carers. Local authorities would be required to assess planning proposals, and the development of commercial and public space, in terms of the ways in which children and their parents, young people, older people, disabled people and carers define their needs. This would involve placing a premium on safe and accessible public spaces, with accessible and affordable transport; and the development of local strategies that integrate issues of work, time, care, space and welfare services (one example of the latter is the 'Time in the City' projects in Modena in Italy, where imaginative, user-centred initiatives have been adopted that integrate the delivery of services with commercial and school opening times). It might also include the encouragement of reciprocal activities in local communities, such as time-banking. Strategies to develop stronger local communities, and to build the kind of local democracy that could determine care needs, would require stable and long-term funding and support for local, rooted, community and self-help groups.

A social environment of care would shift the focus on children and young people away from the idea of 'investment', and towards a respect for them as citizens of the present. The rationale that education is an investment in children provides no basis for attending to the needs of those who may not have an educational future - older people, disabled people and children with learning disabilities. A care orientated approach would involve reframing the testing and target-centred culture of education towards broader values of education as supporting children (or adults) in developing their emotional, physical, intellectual and creative capabilities. Public spaces would be seen as sites of engagement rather than containment. In the current anxiety over children's behaviour, especially towards those in authority, little has been said about the mutual dynamic of respect. Research by Stephen Frosh,

Ann Phoenix and Rob Pattman has demonstrated that teenage boys are acutely aware of being seen as socially and educationally problematic, and of being disparaged by adults; they thus continually invoke a demand for greater respect.[4]

As far as parenting responsibilities are concerned, the central question is not one of the state's enforcement of parents' obligations to care; on the contrary, the question should be *how far society supports a commitment to care*. Enforcing an obligation to care is irrelevant to the majority of parents, who already have a sense of their commitments. Furthermore, the notion that parents should be punished for any transgressions - for example by the withdrawal of their child benefit if their child truants - undermines the principle that child support is a social good. Benefits are there to compensate for the costs of child care rather than to monitor the care itself. Policies around parenting, care, and work/life balance have to be framed in these terms: how do we cherish children? what do we need as individuals and collectivities to fulfil our commitments to others? and how do we enhance equality and respect? This would - crucially - involve measures to combat the gender imbalance in caring responsibilities, but it would also mean attending to the inequalities that arise from lack of access to services - minority ethnic families and those with disabled children are those least well served by family services. Enforcing the obligation on parents would become a secondary issue, and is in any case one that can only be properly developed once we have established the first (supporting the commitment to care).

We also need strategies to enhance paid care work in order to establish and formalise career paths into care work. This would involve developing training for care work that is person-centred rather than task-oriented; based on the practical ethics of everyday life, and on the experiences of those who require support (this would mean, for example, being attentive to people's needs, being non-judgmental; recognising human dignity). It would also involve user groups being more involved in monitoring courses and trainees.

The ethics of care should not simply be about care relations and services; it needs to influence the organisation and management of work, and even of markets, in the manner of ethical environmentalism. This could begin by

4. Stephen Frosh, Ann Phoenix and Rob Pattman, *Young Masculinities*, Palgrave 2002.

developing and showcasing 'care' cultures in high profile work, social and political organisations - such as Parliament, trade unions and large commercial organisations.

By elevating care I do not mean to imply that we simply reward, and therefore reinforce, women's responsibilities to care. With the demise of the male breadwinner and the encouragement of women into paid work we face new and old dilemmas about gender equality policies. One goal is to have a universal caregiver model which would encourage men and women to share care by taking up part-time paid work and part-time care. This would combine shorter and more flexible working hours with informal care and locally organised but publicly supported neighbourhood care centres. But we know that even in Sweden, which has some of these elements in place, the dominance of the male organisation of working time and careers has been difficult to shift, especially in the private sector. It is for this reason that we need to argue not only for policies around time, money and services, but also for a social environment of care seen as part of a long-term vision of universal citizenship. Such a vision would contribute to a more egalitarian, inclusive and interdependent society. Our struggles in the twentieth century were about work; now they have to be about care as well.

The politics of well-being

Hetan Shah

Hetan Shah argues that the politics of well-being contains powerful insights which can inform the left across a range of issues, but there are also potential pitfalls.

It is impossible to read the newspapers each week without stumbling across a new survey on what makes us happy or on which city has the best quality of life. Odd to think, then, that the term 'quality of life' didn't even exist until around fifty years ago, and research shows it had not made it into the dictionaries as late as 1978.

The question of what promotes well-being is galvanising interest much more widely than the occasional surfacing of a survey - often dodgy - in the press. (As usual it is worth looking out for the sponsor. A recent survey sponsored by a travel agent found that holidays made us happy.) Well-being is being taken seriously as a force to inform our politics. The Prime Minister's Strategy Unit (very quietly) produced a paper on the topic of life satisfaction in 2002. At the new economics foundation we produced a *Well-being Manifesto* in 2004. Lord Layard has recently produced a book on the subject of *Happiness*. And in March 2005 the UK government committed to measuring well-being in its new sustainable development strategy. Is happiness politics a trivial middle-class diversion which signals how moribund our political discourse has become? Or is there anything of real value in the politics of well-being? I will argue that the politics of well-being does have the power to be a transformative political force, and has much to offer the left, but that there are also a number of pitfalls that will need to be dealt with.

But, to begin, where has this well-being politics come from? Of course all political philosophies have had more or less implicit conceptions of the good life, so in some ways there is nothing new in this. What informs the current debate is a relatively young strand of academic research which considers the psychology and sociology of what makes people happy and well. Somewhat bizarrely, this stream of research traces back to NASA, who in the 1960s commissioned academics to consider the 'actual or potential wide-ranging impact on our society of the program of space exploration'. Thus was born the Social Indicators Movement, which sought to emulate the perceived success of the postwar economics profession in measuring and intervening in the economy. Over the years the sociologists and psychologists amassed a huge amount of data about our social conditions and how we respond to them. The research comes mostly from large scale survey data, which has been shown to be robust within countries (inter-country comparison is more difficult due to cultural effects). The academics have been working away, holding conferences and writing in their journals (including the serious academic *Journal of Happiness Studies*), but the chasm between academia and policy remains vast. It is only recently that the research has come to the attention of a few UK policy-makers.

Well-being research provides a way of analysing competing claims about policy programmes. Even in this era, focused as it is on 'what works' and evidence-based policy, there is an overwhelming emphasis on proxy indicators. But if we can measure well-being directly, it could help correct our tendency to confuse means and ends. To make this argument clearer, we might take as an example the ways in which decisions are taken about how to measure progress in society.

Politicians focus on GDP growth as the key indicator of progress. But research shows that the relationship between economic growth and well-being has broken down in the richer countries of the world. Thus in the UK in the last thirty years economic output has doubled, but happiness has remained resolutely flat, whilst depression is rising and trust is falling. As Andrew Oswald recently said: 'Some economists and policy-makers will go to their deathbeds ignoring these data. The numbers are too scary. They imply that clever people have for decades given the wrong advice to governments and citizens ... The best evidence now suggests that growth does not work' (*Financial Times*,

17.3.05). The mindset that economic growth is an end rather than a means has powerfully embedded itself in the minds of policy-makers worldwide. A report by the European Commission published in February 2005 indicated the extent to which this is the case when it stated that:

> … the vast majority of European Union citizens do not make a connection between their quality of life and the economic situation in their country. It is therefore necessary to eliminate this discrepancy otherwise it may eventually create a problem when it comes to explaining certain public policies (Special Eurobarometer 215/Wave 62.1).

If reality conflicts with the theory, so much the worse for reality.

What gets counted counts, and policy-makers are still under the sway of economic numbers. One of the key policy conclusions which emerges from research is that we need to measure well-being to see how we are really doing as a society. A systematic set of national well-being accounts could consider levels of happiness and satisfaction, trust, social well-being, meaning and purpose. If we made this the core of how we measured progress, we would live in a radically different society. And all policy could also do a well-being impact analysis. For example, the decision to extend the gambling laws was based on a narrow economic analysis of jobs created (mixed with heavy corporate lobbying). There was little analysis of the impact on well-being, which would probably have led to the opposite outcome.

What does the concept of well-being have to offer the left? Thinking of well-being as one of the true ends of policy, alongside social justice, would enable the left to be more sophisticated in its interventions. Thus we have already seen conceptions of poverty shifting away from purely economic definitions to considerations of whole sets of circumstances, through ideas such as social exclusion. One area that has been largely overlooked, however, is the issue of mental illness, which is extremely detrimental to well-being. Traditional poverty interventions around material redistribution are clearly not enough to deal with mental health problems, which one in six people in the UK suffer from at any time. An analysis based on well-being rather than economics alone could better encompass the needs of those with such problems. Furthermore, raising the well-being of the worst off often requires an approach based on promoting self efficacy rather than one which sees people as passive recipients of welfare. Poverty research is currently moving in this direction, and, for example, Ruth Lister's recent work stresses the desire of the poor to be treated with respect and to have autonomy. But policy practice has yet to catch up.

Well-being research strongly supports the left's traditional redistributive agenda. The evidence is clear: a pound in the pocket of a poor person is worth more in well-being terms than it is in a rich person's. This holds even more strongly across rich and poor nations. But well-being research also provides a nuanced understanding of inequality. Research shows that Europeans are less happy as inequality rises, but this is not the case in the US. This implies that our response to inequality is cultural. In the US inequality tends to reinforce people's belief that they live in a meritocratic society - inequality tends to be seen as reflecting people's different abilities.

But the real power of well-being politics is in helping the left to create a vision of the good life. The left has traditionally been 'deficit focused'; it needs a more positive vision of the good life in post-scarcity societies, where most people do not live in absolute poverty. In the absence of any vision beyond making poorer people richer, a policy vacuum has developed. This vacuum is then filled by the constant call to raise people's material living standards. This is an appropriate strategy for dealing with those in the lowest quintile of income distribution, but it is bizarre when applied to those who are already relatively affluent. There are many more fruitful ways of focusing policy; and areas where well-being research could cast some light on alternatives include work, education, health and sustainable development. Detailed consideration of these can be found in new economics foundation's *Well-being Manifesto*, but here are some of the highlights.

Aspects of the well-being agenda
Work and time

Research shows that our work, both paid and unpaid, is profoundly important for our well-being. Good work can provide us with purpose and challenge, and the opportunity to meet others, and can constitute an important part of our identity. Therefore a well-being economy needs to be concerned with the quality of work in which we engage. There is a growing literature showing what constitutes 'good work'. One of the most important insights in this area has come from the research of Mihaly Csikszentmihalyi into 'flow' - an important contributor to well-being. He defines flow in terms of experiences where we are completely absorbed in what we are doing, and where time feels like it passes very quickly. He argues that we experience flow when we are engaged in activities that are challenging but for which we have the skills to meet the challenge. His research suggests that around 15 per cent of people have never experienced flow, whilst around 20 per cent say they feel it every day, with the rest somewhere in between. The research suggests that work is, in fact, one of the places we are most likely to find flow. We need to think about how to redesign work so that it enables people to flourish and experience flow. The evidence suggests that this is likely to go hand in hand with greater productivity, and would help to deal with the fact that more workplace sickness arises from mental health than any other cause.

Whilst good work can promote well-being, and unemployment is terrible for our happiness, the UK has the longest working hours in Western Europe. Long working hours crowd out some of the key things that the research shows bring well-being: time spent with friends and family, volunteering and doing things in the local community, spending time in the natural environment or engaging in sports and hobbies. A significant proportion of those working long hours are not doing so because they love their work or because they are poor. It is on the mistaken belief that more money and more consumption will bring happiness. In the US, research which has tracked people across time shows that at any given stage most people believe that 20 per cent more income would make them happier. But measuring their life satisfaction a few years later when they have achieved that rise in income shows that they are still no happier - they have adapted to the new level of income. Status effects are also powerful: people are always comparing themselves with others and wanting to get to the top of the pile. But this is a zero sum game in well-being terms as we are fighting for places on a hierarchy - if I'm richer than you then necessarily you are poorer than me.

One of the strongest points that emerges from the well-being research is that we spend too much time chasing money, and not enough time with our friends and family. A vision of the good life for the left needs to grapple with this, building on ideas of thinkers such as André Gorz. One simple mechanism which would begin to deal with this issue would be to allow people to 'buy back' their time from their workplaces: in other words to trade income for working time. More broadly, as a society we should try and take our future productivity increases in the form of time rather than income. This seems to be an emerging phenomenon. A Cambridge University study found that, despite increasing pressures to earn and spend more, over a quarter of British adults aged 30-59 have voluntarily made a long term change in lifestyle that resulted in earning less money. The most common reason for the change was to spend more time with their families. Downshifters were spread fairly evenly across age groups and social grades. The study dispelled the myth that downshifting is confined to middle-aged wealthier individuals who have accumulated substantial assets and can afford the financial risk. Thus many people are already turning against the growing pressures to earn to take back their time - showing that well-being politics is tapping into something quite fundamental.

Education

There is a lack of clarity about what the education system is for. It seems based on a curious mix between two ideas. Firstly there is the concept of the renaissance man, roundly educated in a range of academic subjects. Secondly there is the idea that education is a preparation for your working life in the economy. A well-being focus says that education should promote a flourishing life. It should aim to create capable and emotionally well-rounded young people who are happy and motivated. Research by the new economics foundation found that young people's happiness and curiosity plummeted between primary and secondary school, never to recover. The number of children strongly agreeing to the statement 'I learn a lot at school' dropped from 71 per cent at primary school to 18 per cent at secondary school. We also found that the primary school with markedly the best academic results of the four examined had the lowest levels of happiness and curiosity. This confirms something which we all know: the targets culture in secondary schools is leading to distorted incentives. Rather than promoting pupils' curiosity and personal development, teachers have to maximise grades by teaching to the test.

The academic system is also extremely narrow. The psychologist Howard Gardner showed many years ago that we have a range of 'intelligences' (including musical, spatial, physical, interpersonal and intrapersonal), but that the education system focuses overwhelmingly on the linguistic and mathematical. The Tomlinson report was the turning point at which we failed to turn: Blair ignored the report's proposed reforms to the education and examination system for 14-19 year olds (including a long needed rethink of the A-level system) because of fear about the pre-election perceptions of a small number of middle-class parents in swing seats. We need to broaden the scope of the education system to enhance creativity, social skills and emotional intelligence. How would schools look if the league tables ranked them on the new economics foundation's measures of curiosity and happiness? We need different incentives in place in order to get different results.

Health

There are obvious links between the promotion of health and of well-being. It is becoming increasingly clear that psychological factors influence people's health to a very large degree. One of the most astonishing findings of research in this field is the huge positive influence of happiness on longevity. One piece of evidence for this comes from the nuns study. In the 1930s, a group of young nuns were asked to write a short autobiography. These papers were recently reanalysed in terms of the amount of positive emotions expressed in the writing. A strong relationship was found to exist between the amount of positive emotion expressed (taken as a proxy of well-being) and the longevity of the nuns (who had very similar lifestyles with regard to, for example, diet and living standards). Ninety per cent of the quarter who had expressed the most positive emotion in their autobiographies were still alive at the age of 85, compared to just 34 per cent of the quarter who had expressed the least positive emotion. There is currently some discussion about how the relationship between happiness and longevity actually operates: are happy people less stressed, or, for example, do they look after their bodies better? Whatever the specifics of how it works, however, it is clear that there is a strong relationship between well-being and longevity.

An incredible amount is spent on our 'health' service, but most of it focuses on dealing with physical symptoms of sickness. We need to reconfigure the purpose of the system in order to promote well-being, or what the World Health Organisation calls complete health, which it defines as 'a state of complete physical, mental and social well-being and not merely the absence of disease or infirmity'. It is acknowledged amongst policy-makers that there is a need to shift the system from being treatment oriented to being more prevention focused. Whilst we are taking some steps towards this, we need to accelerate this process. We should invest and commit to disease prevention and public health promotion rather than focusing on technical solutions to ill-health and a 'pill for every ill'. As discussed earlier, mental health promotion is also integral to promoting well-being. The evidence shows that our self perceived health matters far more than our objective health status in terms of our well-being. And promoting overall well-being through a combination of psycho-social interventions will have positive feedback on physical health.

Community

The traditional left model for intervention has focused on the state, and has underestimated the importance of non-state actors, especially communities acting for themselves. In particular, research shows that community engagement not only improves the well-being of those involved but also improves the well-being of others. The relationship is positive in both directions: involvement increases well-being and happy people tend to be more involved in their community. We are social animals: for example, there is the amazing statistic that if you presently do not belong to any group, joining a club or society of some kind halves the risk that you will die in the next year. Government is increasingly seeing the voluntary sector and social enterprise as a means to deliver public services, and funding is following this aim. But this is to underestimate the importance of community organisations, which are essentially social glue. There are a huge number of unincorporated community organisations which are below the radar of government. Increasing support for them is likely to create a powerful well-being multiplier effect.

Sustainable development

The environmental movement has been languishing in the UK for at least the last decade. One reason for this is that its focus upon *limits* has not been something that has commanded popular support. Well-being politics provides the opportunity to revitalise the environmental movement through providing compelling evidence that our present unsustainable lifestyles are not making us any happier. In fact materialistic people (those who believe that money and possessions will make them happier) are less happy than others. Well-being politics creates the space for the discussing the idea that we could move towards a more sustainable lifestyle whilst maintaining or even increasing our quality of life. This could be the most important outcome of any politics of well-being.

There are, however, tensions between individual well-being and sustainable development, which are not always acknowledged. Air travel is a case in point. The language of 'sustainable communities' glibly marries the ideas, but the focus is more on liveability than real sustainability. There are difficult choices to be made, as was also indicated by ippr's Commission on Sustainable Development in the South East. Notably their second working paper was titled 'The problems of success: reconciling economic growth and quality of life in the South East'.

The challenges for a politics of well-being

There are a number of challenges faced by well-being politics.

The first is the mistaken belief that happiness constitutes well-being. We have goals other than happiness which are worth pursuing. The good life is not just about maximising happiness. For example, a freedom fighter may sacrifice everything to fight for the freedom of her country. Or, more prosaically, there is the question of having children. Research suggests that becoming a parent increases levels of meaning and purpose, but decreases life satisfaction. Well-being has at least two dimensions. One is based on happiness and pleasure - life satisfaction is a good indicator of this. The other is more closely aligned to self efficacy, purpose and challenge. The person who climbs a mountain, engages in historical archival research or raises a child does not feel moment-by-moment happiness. Instead she has a sense of self efficacy, and engages with challenge. This comes back to an ancient battle between conceptions of the good life. The hedonic school of thought said that we should maximise pleasure. The eudaimonic said that we should lead flourishing lives, of which pleasure was a part, but that challenge and meaning were crucial.

A second challenge is the mistaken view that the point of politics is solely to maximise well-being - what is known as utilitarianism. Richard Layard argues that he is a utilitarian, and believes in maximising happiness. Happiness and social justice can, however, live in uneasy tension. The key problem is the issue of psychological adaptation. If I am poor or deprived (e.g. due to a disease), but adapt to my condition and am a relatively happy soul, this gives the utilitarian no argument for intervention. And, as discussed earlier, research shows that whilst inequality makes people less happy in Europe, people are happy with it in the US as it confirms to them that they live in a meritocracy. So the utilitarian ethic is not enough to get us to social justice. (Layard in fact cares greatly about inequality, and is mistaken in calling himself a utilitarian: he would approve of situations which help the worst off even if they do not maximise happiness). Similarly, research by MORI shows that ethnic diversity in a locality tends to reduce happiness. The utilitarian conclusion may be to restrict diversity. But our beliefs about freedom, discrimination and fairness tell us that this is wrong. This shows that we care about more than individual well-being, and that the good society does more than simply aim to maximise it. Therefore well-being research needs to be situated in a broader political framework, which is concerned with social justice and environmental sustainability alongside well-being. This is fundamental.

Thirdly and relatedly, well-being research can help to inform the debate, but it cannot provide all the answers. Well-being research is good at setting the direction of policy by reminding us of what contributes to flourishing. It is less good, however, at technical questions of how to best operationalise a certain policy. For example, to create an economy which promotes well-being needs an understanding of political economy and behavioural economics, areas which are outside the scope of well-being research (see for example the article by Andrea Westall in this issue).

There are, then, three questions which well-being research is still grappling with, although each of them is superable. One issue is that of our expectations and ability to adapt. If our expectations always rise as fast as our situations improve, perhaps we can never increase well-being. The question that is occupying well-being research presently is what precisely do we adapt to, and what do we not adapt to. For example, Richard Easterlin has argued that longitudinal studies show that we do not adapt to our friendships and relationships in the same way as we do to our financial situation. These kinds of insights are crucial to forging a politics of well-being.

A further issue that researchers are grappling with is the question of what role culture plays in what gives us well-being. For example, it seems likely that the effect of being made unemployed on well-being is a function of the particular structure of Western industrial societies, where the employment relationship is pervasive and key to our identities. This raises the interesting question for policy-makers of whether to take a particular 'taste' as given, or to seek to change it. This might apply, for example, in relation to the research indicating that happiness is higher in locales which are less ethnically diverse.

Finally, researchers need to deal with the challenge of policy by averages: how far are the constituents of well-being universal and how far do they vary for individuals? Even if the average person gets well-being from their relationships and community, what about the odd outliers, for example, who genuinely want to spend all their time working? This is the liberal challenge to some of the more paternalistic formulations of well-being politics. Therefore, alongside needing to be pretty sure about what causes well-being, and confident that policy can be effective in making a difference, we also need to try to formulate policy in such a way that it does not unduly restrict people's choices. This might lead to what some American academics have described as a 'libertarian paternalism', where people are guided to make the 'right choice' but are always given the opportunity to make other choices. For example, it has been shown that default options are very important: when people are given the option to opt into a company pension, far fewer join than if they have to opt out. These kinds of techniques can be used to create policy which makes the 'right' choice the easy choice.

The future of well-being politics

The politics of well-being is likely to become more and more powerful. Unlike some traditional left politics, it is resonant with what people want and care about. It is also aspirational, unlike environmental politics, which is perceived as being about limits. It will take time to embed, as politicians are naturally frightened of tabloid headlines along the lines of 'government concerned about Britain's happiness'. This was an important factor in the low profile given to the Strategy Unit's paper on life satisfaction.

Nevertheless, well-being is being taken up in a range of places. Most prominently, the new UK sustainable development strategy *Securing the Future* committed to exploring how policies might change 'with an explicit well-being focus', and to developing more comprehensive well-being indicators. These well-being indicators will be powerful symbols of what we care about as a society (echoing the Bhutanese desire to want to promote Gross National Happiness rather than Gross National Product). Indicators are also powerful facilitators of change in society. Once we measure something we can analyse causation, change behaviour and continue to check how we are faring.

Local government is grappling with well-being, having been given a broad power to promote economic, social and environmental well-being by the Local Government Act 2000. The power has largely been treated with confusion, but there are emerging examples of creative uses, including smart procurement which meets social goals simultaneously with economic considerations. In Scotland, Dumfries and Galloway is presently piloting indicators of needs satisfaction and well-being in order to refocus the health system around well-being rather than sickness.

At the regional level, some of the Regional Development Agencies are giving serious consideration to the implications of the well-being research, with the East Midlands Development Agency at the forefront, having commissioned thinking on alternative measures of progress.

Academic research in this area is being taken more seriously, and therefore is likely to become more well resourced and significant. For example, in the US there is now a powerful Positive Psychology network, whose aim is to focus psychology on flourishing rather than on illness. And in the UK, Bath University has a large ESRC programme considering well-being in developing countries.

The politics of well-being has articulate proponents, resonance amongst the public and genuinely new political insights to offer. Everybody cares about quality of life, and there is growing awareness that this rests on far more than economic considerations. Therefore well-being politics is situated to inform where we go next. What remains at stake, however, is whether or not this will be in a broader political framework that takes social justice and environmental sustainability seriously. I am an optimist about the future of well-being politics, but a pessimist about the politics of social justice or environmental sustainability - the broader political framework of the good life.

Economics as if people mattered

Andrea Westall

Andrea Westall suggests alternative ways of thinking about economics.

Following an election focused more on single issues and delivery than values and passion, there is a need to recreate a politics of the left based on a strong narrative that both inspires and provides the basis or framework for action. Core to this challenge is the development of a political economy and economic policies that are able to deliver on a clear vision of society and the good life, harnessed to meet people's and society's needs, and within environmental constraints. That is easy to say but there is surprisingly little current debate on this issue.

Writers on the left attack New Labour for not having a coherent values-based economic policy, and for being too uncritical of the role of business and markets in delivering on (or preventing the delivery of) core left objectives. The third way was obviously an attempt to try to set out a coherent vision for a revived social democracy set within the perceived 'limits' of globalisation on national decision-making and control, and the problems of centralised delivery. Many commentators have noted its weak analysis and acceptance of the benign nature of modern capitalism, particularly global capital flows, and therefore its inability to deal with their consequences.

This article is not going to attempt to define a new political economy; its aim, rather, is to explore alternative economic traditions and thinkers who are only occasionally picked up by the left. These different perspectives see economic activity as encompassing much more than traditional areas such as paid work, or investment in capital, and focus primarily on how the good life can be delivered through wider, or different, concepts of wealth, work, money or capital. They also challenge us to create new ways to get back in control of the economic system at all levels from local to global and, by offering different understandings of how economies work in practice, potentially suggest new and more effective ways to do so.

New Labour has an economic policy but it does not have a political economy. Its economic policy has been remarkably effective in creating stability, keeping inflation low, and underpinning high employment. It sees economic growth - pursued chiefly through promoting entrepreneurship, innovation and productivity - as central to increasing quality of life and opportunity, providing jobs, supporting the provision of quality public services, and (but rather quietly) enabling the redistribution of income to tackle poverty. Concern over future pension provision and threats to UK competitiveness from overseas producers ensures that this approach is hard to challenge, since to do so could be to risk competitiveness and growth, leading to unemployment and reduced tax take.

But there are clearly problems that are not being answered, and cannot be answered, by the narrow focus on economic growth and productivity. Inequality remains high, both within the UK and internationally. Poverty persists, yet there are cries for work-life balance that reflect overwork - in a society that once expected that economic growth would bring more leisure time and a secure retirement. Crude measures of progress such as GDP are not correlated with measures of wellbeing (which remains static): this is partly a reflection of the way in which economic growth creates 'bads' as well as goods for individuals, communities and the environment. Climate change is a particular problem for current economic policy frameworks; they are an inappropriate means for addressing the scale and fundamental nature of the issues involved. And when mainstream economists such as Joseph Stiglitz start to argue that the global economy is becoming potentially more unstable, or strongly question the positive impacts of free trade, it's clearly time for a rethink.

Other commentators, including many in *Soundings*, point to the erosion in public values and public goods brought about by creeping marketisation, and the reduction in time and inclination for civic activity that results from individualisation and overwork. And, despite some efforts towards joined-up government, our fragmented approach to policy-making - focusing on separate issues such as housing, transport, productivity, climate change - fails to deal with conflicting targets and the complex interactions between social, economic and environmental issues. Economic thinking and practice seems to remain resolutely separate from social and environmental policy, making it impossible to explore in more than a tokenistic way the inevitable synergies, interconnections and trade-offs that a more integrated approach would bring.

Part of the reason we are in this situation is the dominance of neoclassical economic thinking and influence over practice. That hold has become embedded not only in our politicians and policy-makers but within media, general culture and conversation. Edward Fullbrook, in his article on Post-Autistic Economics in *Soundings* 29, set out the problems of an approach focused on an inappropriate view of human nature, an incorrect analysis of the dynamics of firms or markets, and an inability to cope with environmental constraints. Another aspect of the problem is that elements of economic activity, such as capital flows and credit creation, have become increasingly divorced from any form of public control.

Any approach to political economy has to deal with and understand a highly complex reality. Anti-globalisation movements have successfully raised issues that many politicians would rather avoid; but, equally, the tendency of some to focus on tangible 'evil' targets misses the point that we are dealing with a dynamic system of incentives and interactions (many of which make sense in isolation - though of course certain institutions, such as the IMF, are underpinned by a narrow neoclassical approach to economics that doesn't actually make sense). Faced with all this, the choices are either to jump in and try to deal with it all; to continue to offer piecemeal approaches; or to bow down to the inevitability of current economic forces - as with Dostoevksy, in *Notes from the Underground*, you can

> ... sink voluptuously into inertia, silently and impotently gnashing your teeth and reflecting that there isn't even anybody for you to be angry with, that an object for your anger can't even be found, and perhaps never will be ... and consequently there remains only the same outcome, which is banging one's head as hard as one can against the stone wall.

But rather than giving in, we need to look at alternative approaches to economics, which can help in opening up new ways to look at existing problems, particularly since some adopt values which resonate with a left perspective. Ecological economics, for example, focuses not only on environmental constraints but also on values such as social justice, wellbeing and more participative democratic processes. The left has up until now avoided integrating an analysis of the environment with issues of social justice and equality, but this evasion cannot continue.

The problem is, however, that these analyses tend to stop short of practical policy solutions or a coherent political economy. So as a way of framing these discussions and providing inspiration for a new sense of purpose, we can also look to a range of thinkers who have often been bypassed - from co-operative socialist or liberal or even green backgrounds. We desperately need, as Schumacher (one of the core inspirations for the new economics foundation) has argued, an economics 'as if people mattered'.

Looking back and outwards for inspiration

Karl Polanyi, an Austrian economic historian, is a useful starting point for breaking out of our usual ways of thinking about economics and our current model of capitalism (see, for example, his *The Great Transformation, The Political and Economic Origins of Our Time*, first published in 1944). His discussion of economic systems goes far beyond a focus on markets, or on the pros and cons of capitalism, or the relative balance of market or state-led production and delivery. He sees economic activity as based on three economic principles: market-based exchange, redistribution and reciprocity. This thicker understanding of economic activity enables us to think more widely about the importance of productive work that is unpaid, such as care, or the informal distribution and mutual aid between people that is in effect the bedrock of society. Economic measures of growth and progress such as GDP do not include the outcomes of productive individual and community activity which is unpaid, thus implicitly undermining and devaluing activity which may be core to creating wellbeing and social justice.

Polanyi also breaks us out of the trap of inevitability, by pointing out that the dominance of market-based transactions is only recent: it was the 'great transformation' of the Industrial Revolution that began the process of weakening a more moral economy based on need. He reminds us that economic activity is never free-floating and uncontrollable but is always embedded in society.

But economic and market control need not mean control by central government. Apart from the centralised Marxist or Fabian models of socialism, other traditions of co-operative socialism, along with parts of liberal and green thought, suggest other ways of understanding and managing economic production, ownership and distribution. At the heart of this analysis is the idea that economic activity should be empowering, values-based, and subject to broader and decentralised democratic control, implying new governance and organisational models. The revived interest in mutualism draws on this strand of economic and political organisation.

John Stuart Mill, a liberal, argued for a co-operative capitalism, in a fairly similar way to socialists such as Ruskin, who set out a vision of a co-operative socialism where much of industry would be run on a mutual basis. Ruskin also focused on the human experience of economic activity and how this related to the good life. He argued that there is 'no wealth but life' and that economic activity has become an end in itself not a means, impoverishing society and individuals in the process. His words in *Unto this Last*, published in 1862, still make sense:

> A nation cannot last as a money-making mob: it cannot with impunity, it cannot with existence - go on despising literature, despising nature, despising science, despising art, despising compassion and concentrating its soul on Pence.

Ruskin believed that work should support and enhance life. In other words, the focus should not be entirely on the quantity of work (even in its broadest sense) but also on its quality.

It is interesting that when Ivan Illich, a maverick Austrian writer and thinker, argued in the 1970s that our economic system and model of top-down government and education denies personal empowerment, confidence and skill, he was criticised by the left. He argued that consumption creates passivity and that more emphasis should be put on supporting the retention of diverse human cultures, and supporting self-reliant local economies which encompass more shared activity. He saw consumer society as 'serfdom' and challenged people to choose:

> a life of action over a life of consumption, which will enable us to be spontaneous, independent, yet related to each other, rather than maintaining a lifestyle which only allows to make and unmake, produce and consume - a style of life which is merely a way station on the road to the depletion and pollution of the environment.

He suggested new institutions and processes which he called 'tools for conviviality'.[1] These included skills exchanges, models of decentralised learning, and ways of creating health outside medical intervention – ideas which prefigured current debates around lifelong learning, and the idea of healthy communities where citizens help to create their own health. This recognition of the need to create a strong collective public realm, linked to and creating thriving local economies, needs greater attention from the left.

This analysis, alongside ideas from Buddhism and Ghandi, led E. F. Schumacher to try to create economic theory and practice at a scale which did not impoverish people or community wellbeing, and was not environmentally unsustainable.[2] Schumacher was behind the concept of intermediate technology, proposing productive technologies which were cheap, suitable for small-scale application, and 'compatible with man's need for creativity'. People could be freed from paid labour and dependency, becoming their own employers, or members of co-operatives working for local production; this would create a 'progressive decentralisation of population, of political and economic power', as well as more satisfying lives, where the aim was the maximum of welfare with the minimum of consumption.

If your inclination is to dismiss this kind of vision as utopian and impractical, stop and think of the trends towards people working for themselves or downshifting (at least for the affluent), as well as concern over the loss of core local services. There has been a great deal of support from a diverse range of

---

1. The core ideas can be found in E. F. Schumacher's *Small is Beautiful: A study of economics as if people mattered.*
2. M. Max-Neef, *Human Scale Development*, 1987.

people for the new economics foundation's (nef) work on 'ghost town' and 'clone town' Britain, which highlights the loss of local services and dominance by powerful monopolistic retailers, and for proposals by others for collective land ownership in order to provide the underpinning for greater community control over local economic services, housing and public space. Such ideas clearly resonate with a widespread concern over the direction of our society, and about the loss of control over our ability to meet basic needs and generate some level of personal and collective security.

E conomic policy and thinking should pause and think about the impact of scale. For example, the current obsession with the large scale in procurement by the public sector misses the potentially positive impacts of more local and smaller-scale delivery on struggling local economies, as well as their more positive environmental impacts. The pursuit of scale derives from a focus on narrowly conceived and measured concepts of competitiveness and productivity.

Much of this thinking is underpinned by a concept of needs that goes beyond the Maslow hierarchy where subsistence comes first. Max-Neef, renowned for his 'barefoot economics' and human-scale development, proposed nine fundamental needs: subsistence, protection, affection, understanding, participation, creation, recreation, identity and freedom; these can be satisfied through being, having, doing and interacting.[3] This thinking underpins Hetan Shah's analysis, in this issue of *Soundings*, of the potential in taking wellbeing as central to the good life and to the goals of policy-making. It is also creates a framework which enables us to consider whether different kinds of economic activity or economic policy may or may not satisfy these needs.

Drawing on this broad canvas, thinkers like James Robertson have tried to create a coherent framework for thinking differently about economics. Robertson argues for a SHE economy - sane, humane and ecological - based on a number of principles, including:

♦ Systematic empowerment of people and communities to take control of their own futures and be more economically self-reliant (particularly in order to create built-in buffering - but not isolation - from external economic conditions)

---

3. A good summary of James Robertson's views and ideas can be found in J. Robertson, *Transforming Economic Life: A Millennial Challenge*, Schumacher Briefings (1) 1998.

+ Conservation of resources and the environment
+ Evolution to a 'decentralised multi-level one-world economic system' rather than one based on nation states
+ Restoration of political and ethical choice into economic thought and practice.[4]

Robertson, like many similar thinkers, is not anti-market, but he argues that economic institutions and prices need to appropriately incentivise the 'right' behaviour. His core argument is that the self-reinforcing cycle of consumption growth, production growth and money growth needs to be broken, based as it is on a employer-centred and producer-led economy rather than a people-centred or citizen-centred model.

He adopts a systemic analysis that recognises the need for a framework of reinforcing incentives and institutions rather than just isolated solutions. These would include, for example:

+ Introducing a citizens' income, increasing with age, which would replace tax benefits and welfare in order to recognise the equal entitlement of all to resources, to support unpaid work and civic activity, and to reduce poverty traps.
+ Restructuring the tax system (at all levels from local to global) away from productive activity and towards bads (environmental resource use) and unproductive assets (for example, land). Part of this thinking is based on Henry George (who inspired Georgist economics), who argued that, since no productive effort has gone into creating land, it should not be owned, and that those that do own it should be charged rent. This rent or tax would reduce speculative activity, and would ensure that all gains from public activity or individual effort in adding value to land would go back to the public rather than into the pockets of the landowners. (Driven by a need for new sources of taxation, this idea of taxing unearned wealth from land has recently become a focus of interest - for example in the case of transport developments in London.)

---

4. For a sweeping and fascinating view of these developments, see A. Evers and J.L. Laville, *The Third Sector in Europe*, 2004.

- Developing more self-reliant economies, which reduce the need to travel and are not totally dependent on paid economic activity.
- Developing new indicators to measure a more realistic and humane form of progress.
- Public purchasing policies which incentivise equitable and sustainable practice.
- Education not just for work but also to support life as an active citizen.
- A new and powerful system of international governance to address the complex challenges of, for example, trade, and its impacts on international development, local economic viability, and environmental sustainability.

A core issue for Robertson, which can only be sketched out here, is that of rethinking the money system. He argues that the requirement for interest payments fuels unsustainable growth, reinforced by the unregulated way in which banks can issue new money. He also argues that a single currency can severely affect different parts of an economy, and therefore advocates multiple currencies to create more stability, and to keep and develop purchasing power within local economies. He argues that a global currency would also be desirable, in order to remove the perverse hold of the dollar on the world economy, which, in effect, enables the US to continue to consume beyond its means, further fuelling unsustainable growth and instability. These ideas create another perspective on a single European currency, and the idea that any regional economic variations can *just* be dealt with through a redistribution of resources.

A central theme running through many approaches is that of promoting more economic democracy through institutional transformation. Whilst this is often presumed to apply only to business activity, it is also relevant more broadly. In particular, there is a role for the third sector here. In the UK, like the US, the third sector has tended to be seen as a means for responding to government or market failure, rather than as an alternative or complementary source of economic activity. The European concept of social economy is more capable of capturing this role. Recently there have been increasing numbers of hybrid organisational models: multi-stakeholder social enterprises that involve market activity, voluntary commitment, and mutual production and decision-making, and create collective wealth while delivering trust-based services. These organisations engage a range of different stakeholders in complex governance and decision-making models (sometimes including the state) and could be seen as new spaces for power, democracy and resource allocation.[5] We could very profitably look at the implications here, not only for a strong social economy to underpin jobs and communities, but for lessons on wider institutional and business reform. These practical innovations also draw on veins of thinking (for example in France) around a more civic or solidarity based economy.

Taking a different view of economics

In *Soundings 29* Edward Fullbrook offered an account of the ways in which alternative or heterodox economics have been sidelined by the power of 'mainstream' neoclassical economics. He also noted how this dominant thinking affects policy-making, for example by preventing recognition of people's complex and ethical decision-making processes, or of the challenges and implications of sustainable development.

The ICAPE website (International Confederation of Associations of Pluralism in Economics) lists many sources for different 'economics', including institutional, feminist, social, ecological, evolutionary, Georgist, post-Keynesian or behavioural (see www.econ.tcu.edu/econ/icare/main.html). Each has its own scope, but as the Post-Autistic Economics (PAE) movement emphasises, the aim should be for pluralism. So what have heterodox or alternative economics to contribute to a left political economy or policy-making?

Behavioural economics enables us to challenge some of the assumptions guiding current policy-making that prevent radically different approaches, for example the argument for marketisation on the grounds that non-market mechanisms are not 'efficient'. Thus behavioural economics points to the unsurprising evidence that people can make decisions that are not self-seeking but are in fact fair. Equally, there is evidence that monetary rewards are not always motivating: for instance, paying volunteers can reduce their willingness to engage. This kind of research proves that people do respond

---

5. For further practical implications of behavioural economics, see *Behavioural Economics: The 7 principles of human behaviour for policymakers*, available from www.neweconomics.org.

to motivations other than simple self-interest, and underpins broader views of economic activity that incorporate reciprocity or altruism. Another example of the difficulties inherent in relying on purely monetary incentives to promote effective outcomes can be seen in the problems that have arisen in attempting to motivate all teachers through performance-related pay.[6]

Institutional economics recognises the importance of social norms and institutions in framing economic outcomes and decision-making. This suggests that alternative systems of reinforcing laws, institutions and social norms could be designed, for example systems that can support and encourage equitable and environmental economic activity. One useful outcome of this approach would be to prove once and for all that organisational models other than shareholder companies can be effective in achieving societal goals, given the correct set of incentive and governance structures. It can also demonstrate that introducing competition does not always guarantee enhanced outcomes for end users. For example, limited thinking about competition led to the fallacious assumption that the opening up of directory enquiries would inevitably result in cheaper prices and better services for choice-loving consumers.

Evolutionary economics recognises that economies and markets are not static; they develop over time and do not tend towards some equilibrium level, as is assumed in the self-organising principle of neoclassical economics. Rather, because they are a function of different actors (for example, individuals, firms, civil society associations, sectors, states) as well as norms and rules, they create outcomes that cannot easily be predicted. The dynamics of the system come from connections and interactions between actors. With the increasing understanding of the nature of complexity and the development of soft systems approaches adapted to complex social reality, this kind of analysis has become more sophisticated. Various rule-based modelling approaches, such as agent and multi-agent based modelling, are being used to investigate the evolution of economies and the impacts of policy interventions.

These insights reinforce and explain the reasons why an economics of command and control cannot work in many circumstances. Jake Chapman's

---

6. See J. Chapman, *System Failure: Why governments must learn to think differently*, Second Edition, Demos 2004.

brilliantly accessible analysis of systems thinking applied to policy-making illustrates the implications: chiefly that the search for a single solution is often not possible and needs to be replaced by creating appropriate processes and learning systems that can be framed with values and objectives.[7]

Ecological economics has perhaps the most to say to a left approach to economics, seeking to combine a focus on wellbeing, environmental sustainability and justice within a common framework. Core to the foundations of ecological economics is a focus on people, and their needs over time, but within the confines of the limits of environmental resources and the 'carrying capacity' of the biosphere to cope with waste products. Capital is seen as a broader concept, encompassing financial, human, environmental and social. Ecological economists argue that sustainable development is a more appropriate concept than economic growth, since it focuses more on the goals of economic activity (rather than growth per se), as well as on social and intergenerational equity.

Herman Daly, a highly influential and accessible ecological economist, has set out certain core principles of ecological economics, such as the need to recognise the appropriate scale of an economy relative to the ecosystem, and the need for equitable distribution of resources and income; these require complex property rights from the individual to collective and global.[8] He advocates the concept of the steady-state economy, which focuses not on maximising consumption but on minimising 'throughput' - resources and generation of wastes. He is not anti-market, arguing only that resource use should be controlled, not that innovation and entrepreneurship cannot happen within those constraints.

Robert Constanza, writing in the same book, argues that the way to integrate the three goals of ecological sustainability, social fairness and economic efficiency, and to determine their relative value, is to 'get on with the process of value formation and analysis in as participatory and democratic a way as possible, but one which also takes advantage of the full range and depth of scientific information we have accumulated'. A core challenge is that of creating

7. See, for example, his essay in Edward Fullbrook's edited collection, *A Guide to What's Wrong with Economics*, Anthem Press 2004.
8. See for example the wealth of thought in R. Krishnan, J. Harris and N. Goodwin, *A Survey of Ecological Economics* 1995.

analytical tools that allow a more pluralistic model of decision-making and policy design, based on comparing the different values of aspects of a situation, going beyond the purely financial. Cost-benefit analysis (CBA), the usual way of deciding on policy, reduces everything to a monetary equivalent that can be compared. Alternative approaches to such methods include multi-criteria decision analysis, which enables broader notions of value and more participatory decision-making.

This and other new techniques provide some interesting ways through some of the main challenges in balancing economic, social and environmental issues.[8] Other proposals include new measures of progress that account for what is called 'uneconomic' growth, i.e. growth which involves environmental or social costs (such as the costs of dealing with pollution or resource depletion, or the costs of income inequality). One example is the MDP (Measure of Domestic Progress) developed by Tim Jackson for nef, which is currently being considered regionally; the east midlands development agency (emda) is presently conducting a feasibility study (see www.neweconomics.org). This approach can be supplemented by satellite accounts in sectors that enable a more targeted development of appropriate incentive frameworks (for example, they are used in Norway for energy, and land use).

Another example is HEEDnet, a group of heterodox economists involved in ecological, behavioural and institutional economics, focused on designing effective policies to deal with environmental issues (see www.heednet.org). They look at questions such as the ways in which changes in consumer behaviour relate to norms, or public good arguments, or others' behaviour, and explore how understanding such relationships could inform the creation of social institutions that could contribute to public goods, or reinforce positive behaviour.

There is a long way to go in developing these concepts. Other critical resources that are urgently needed include an international trade theory that recognises equity and environmental issues; new theory and practice for the firm; and new understandings of ways of creating the appropriate frameworks for markets.

Moving forwards

The new economics foundation arose out of The Other Economics Summit (TOES) held in 1984. nef's first chair, George McRobie, summarised some of the implications of another way of looking at economics, work, and life as follows:

> The answers to emerge will entail new ways of organising work and meeting human needs, and of guaranteeing incomes; a new emphasis on economic self-reliance, including local economic regeneration and enrichment of poor countries through self-reliant development strategies rather than increasing third world dependence; new awareness of ecological constraints, of human needs for survival, social justice and self-fulfilment, and new economic concepts to take these into account; new growth areas for economic activity in energy-efficient and resource-conserving industries and in care and maintenance of the built and natural environment.

One of the main messages of this summary for the left is that much of this analysis echoes a more co-operative socialism, which can be uncomfortable for those used to a more centralised model. But this political space is increasingly attracting people ; and it offers the scope for a vision for the left which can argue effectively for appropriate methods of control over economic activity, but is at the same time socially liberal and pluralistic in its vision of more empowered and self-reliant people, communities and economies.

Alternative economics stresses the need for strong economic frameworks and incentives that recognise environmental resource impacts alongside social justice, particularly at the global level. But the key challenge, of course, is an understanding of how change can happen in ways which resonate widely enough, and do not raise (or can deal with) the fear of creating economic instability. Ecological economics is beginning to show how we could do this, but it needs much greater practical development. As a result we will have to rethink our core values as well as some core issues and concepts - such as the nature of property rights and 'work', our tax and finance system, our model and frameworks for growth and trade, and the design of international, national and local governance.

There is a huge amount of work to be done. I can feel that headache coming on again, and the pull of Dostoevsky, but for now I'm willing to have a go.

Buy your own job, own your own life

Molly Scott Cato

Molly Scott Cato argues that we need to take more control of our working lives.

The term 'ownership' is a popular buzzword in contemporary management speak, in which usage it has no connection with genuine ownership, but rather means a willingness amongst employees to pay lip-service to their corporate mission statement. Alongside this rise in popularity of phoney ownership, what we have actually seen is a loss of autonomy by employees over their work, and an increasing loss of control of their workplace to global financial interests. In this article I argue both for a regaining of physical control of the workplace through the expansion of cooperatives, and for a shaking off of the ideological dependence on work which provides such valuable support for capitalism as an economic system. These two arguments can be seen as addressing the two fundamental needs of a decent employment system: for job security and job satisfaction. The following sections propose some possible solutions to the problems of work, over-work and workplaces: moving towards cooperative workplaces; reducing our dependence on the money economy and our standards; and changing our ideas about what we need to live a happy life.

Cracking the values code

For many in this late stage of capitalism, work is focused around a corporation whose ownership pattern is unclear and may change frequently. As the recent film *The Corporation* makes clear, this removes the need for any sense of personal responsibility between employer and employee. It also means that the people really pulling the strings are on neither end of that traditional relationship, but rather disconnected shareholders. Their involvement in the 'business' is purely and simply financial.

Globalisation is a process designed to minimise within the process of money-making any remaining involvement with 'stuff'. The simultaneous development of trade liberalisation and financial liberalisation was no coincidence. Globalisation is merely the latest and most blatantly profiteering phase of an economic system that is not called *capitalism* for nothing: As Hutchinson et al point out, the finance industry lies at the heart of globalisation. Ninety-five per cent of the total international transactions of a trillion or so dollars that take place each day are purely financial: 'Globalisation is not about trade; it is about money'.[1]

The consequences of this exclusive focus on money are disastrous for unprotected regional economies, or national economies operating without a powerful currency to back them up. In their account of the devastating effect of the quest for shareholder value on the regional economies of the UK, Martin and Minns identify finance as the key driver. As they argue, the financial system now completely dominates the real economy of goods and services.[2]

In this highly monetised economy, businesses operate on debt, and the greater their ability to take risks - especially financial risks - the more successful are the entrepreneurs. This is how we arrive at the paradoxical situation where the most successful companies are those that sport the largest debts. Halliburton, with its $998m debt, was a shining example of the trend until it managed to save itself through the large contracts it gained in post-war Iraq. Things were not always so cosy for the US administration's favourite corporation. With confidence shattered following the attacks on the Twin Towers, debts at the kinds of levels they were sustaining appeared to be unsupportable. Two months after the attacks, Enron's massive debts came home

---

1. F. Hutchinson, M. Mellor and W. Olsen, *The Politics of Money*, Pluto 2002, p5.
2. R. Martin and R. Minns, 'Undermining the Financial Basis of Regions: The Spatial Structure and Implications of the UK Pension Fund Industry', *Regional Studies*, 29 1995, p128.

to roost (estimates vary, but $20 billion seems a conservative figure, and this was backed by only $2bn of assets). The huge growth rates at Enron, from nowhere to the seventh largest corporation in the US in just fifteen years, had only been possible on the basis of this sort of ungrounded, loan-based strategy. So it became the largest collapse in US history - until the next one.

The next one could have been Halliburton, which had used the same technique of 'unbilled receivables' to inflate the profits it reported to shareholders and the stock-market. The two companies shared many similarities: their place in the energy sector, vast borrowing, and close political ties with the White House. Like Enron, Halliburton had postponed losses and counted money they had not even invoiced as revenue, according to the pressure group Judicial Watch; they overstated profits to the value of $445m during 1999 to 2001. Living on the accounting edge like this might have worked during the boom of the 1990s, but it was becoming impossible in the insecure new century, especially once the foundations of the corporate world were cracked by the World Trade Centre attack and the fall of Enron.

So why is so it so important to inflate the value of your company ('future value captured in the form of market capitalisation', to quote Anderson's gambler's guide to the economy)?[3] It is because critics who describe unregulated global capitalism as a giant casino are not using an analogy. What determines the share value, and therefore the equity, of a globally traded corporation is its perceived value. So Halliburton is only worth what people think it is worth. Thus accounts that overstate the value of a company actually help to increase its value. The real value of many companies, in terms of the assets they possess and could sell on to creditors if they crashed, is a fraction of their nominal stock-market value. So investors, including the banks and insurance companies that invest the money we may have saved, are competing with each other to bid up the price of these companies. If confidence is lost the share value may plummet drastically.

This transformation of the stock-market into a casino has had devastating consequences on our regional economies. A case study of a closure of one locally owned business was carried about by Andy Pike, who researched the

3. B.D. Libert, S.S. Samek and R.E.S. Boulton [all Anderson accountants], *Cracking the Value Code: How Successful Businesses are Creating Wealth in the New Economy* HarperBusiness 2000.

loss of control of a family brewery on the River Wear in Sunderland. The Vaux Brewery was a key local employer, and had been operating since 1837. But globalisation, with its combination of consolidation and monetisation, forced the Nicholson family, who had run the company for three generations, into a flotation on the stock-market. The Nicholsons subsequently struggled unsuccessfully to maintain control of the brewery. As Pike argues, the increases in capital and scale intensity within the brewing industry had created a necessity for investment capital at levels that simply could not be met by retained earnings, or from investment by North East regional investors. In his memoirs, Nicholson identifies the culture clash between traditional and globalising capitalists. As Pike comments, 'the post-"Big Bang" political economy and culture of speculative short-termism, fee-seeking and deal-making by "plain spivs" was increasingly at odds with the Chairman's "gentlemanly capitalism"'.[4]

Readers of *Soundings* are unlikely to have much sympathy for the patriarchal capitalists of the pre-globalisation era, but the loss of security of employment for the workforce, and to the economy as a whole, is clear in this example. Economic decisions are now being made by city dealers seeking only money, with a loss to all players in the economy who are not shareholders. It is no longer enough just to make profits; a fund manager must now make more profits faster - and more profits faster than the fund manager next door. There is cut-throat competition for capital, with success measured in terms of real or perceived shareholder value.

Readers are equally unlikely to have sympathy for Marks & Spencer, whose recent problems are a result of their refusing to play the latest corporate game - rather than competing on price alone, they continued to rely on an ethical commitment to preserve British suppliers and maintain high quality standards. The City did not approve. Stock-market pressure has now resulted in the transfer of M&S supply contracts to the Far East and Eastern Europe, and away from suppliers like Dewhirsts in the Welsh Valleys, which had previously been supported by M&S's 'buy British' policy. This pressure came in spite of an apparent turnaround in the company's fortunes as recently as late 2003, when announced profits had risen by 7 per cent to

---

4   A.J. Pike, '"Shareholder Value" versus the Regions: the Closure of the Vaux Brewery in Sunderland', working paper 2004, pp12, 19.

£311.5m for the six months to September. In the globalised economy, shareholder pressure can make or break companies, and executives are under increasing pressure to generate constantly increasing profits.

Of course companies that are highly indebted are vulnerable not only to their shareholders, but also to the banks who own their debt-equity, and thus to some extent the companies themselves. The nature of this ownership by creditors is made clear when failing companies are offered 'debt-for-equity swaps'. This particular scheme was invented in the 1980s as a neo-imperialist response to the inability of Latin American countries to pay their foreign debts. The collapse of the economies of whole countries would have destroyed the teetering international financial system, so the lenders had as much incentive to find a solution as the borrowers. In this case they found a solution which involved their taking ownership of national assets in return for cancelling some part of the debt. The countries would have been better advised to renege on the debt, as Argentina has recently done in an attempt to find a way out of its recurring financial crisis. (Argentina's politicians appear to have learned from their bruising experience of the global financial markets. In January 2005 the country offered its foreign creditors 25 cents per dollar for the debts. This is effectively a default, but 700,000 bondholders may have to settle for it. The experience may offer a lesson to other indebted national economies around the world.)

A revised version of this debt-for-equity scheme is now being offered to companies whose risk-taking entrepreneurs have failed to convince shareholders that the company is good for the debt, leading to the threat of bankruptcy. At this point the bank can generously step in and agree to take on stock in the company to the value of its loan. While such 'corporate restructuring' is often seen as benign, since it at least prevents the loss of the company, in reality it represents a switch in wealth from shareholders to banks, since in the swap the value at which the stock is exchanged is usually a fraction of its former value. In the case of Marconi, 'rescued' by the 'merciful hands of its bankers' in late 2002, the shareholders lost around 99 per cent of their investment (*Guardian*, 22.8.02).

A debt-for-equity swap at the tourist company My Travel recently provided a welcome windfall for hedge-fund manager Roddy Campbell of Cross Asset Management, as the account below shows:

Typically long/short funds are able to take advantage of debt-for-equity swaps [...], said Campbell. 'You needed to be a distressed fund prepared to take the equity risk ... to really get it', he added. Cross bought My Travel bank debt at 82 in December. Bank debt holders are receiving 88 per cent of the equity in the reorganised company, and the debt is now valued at approximately 180 ... Cross is not alone in having profited from My Travel recently ... London Titanium Capital also held a long bank debt position in the company (*European Hedge Fund Manager News*, 4.3.05).

Thus money can be made simply through gambling on the value of different companies, and trading in their debt. If you work for a publicly traded company your job security may turn out to be at the whim of a city wideboy hustling in the relative values of other companies' debts.

In a highly monetised economy, employment is the only source of security for most people; hence my wish in this section to outline the insecurity of that relationship in the private sector. The public sector is now also coming under pressure that will lead to employment insecurity for many, with critiques of its levels of efficiency (often narrowly conceived in terms of labour costs), and the rates of the taxation that fund it. This pressure is coming particularly from Europe, where the Eurozone countries with their strong public sectors are facing a monetary squeeze; the 'Lisbon agenda', with GATS at its heart, is forcing competition onto the public sector in all member states, often from poor-quality rivals who pay low wages and operate with inferior employment conditions.

Work-life balance or work-profit balance?

So much for job security. What about job satisfaction? Discussions about job satisfaction have been replaced in recent years by a concern for the work-life balance. This assumes immediately that there is a tension between work and life, that one is an unpleasant necessity from which we aim to escape to the other, the sanctuary of the life. I offer as evidence of the unsatisfactory nature of this debate a recent television advert for Thomson holidays, during which we watch a lone, poolside sunbather repeatedly shifting his sun-lounger to catch every possible ray, while we are informed that 'for every afternoon in the sun you have to work three weeks and two days'. There are a number of points about the image conveyed by this advert that are both symbolic and deeply troubling. First, *the man is on his own*. Are we to assume that he prefers spending his holidays alone, that his perfect escape is to a place where there is only his own company? Second, he is sitting by a swimming pool and yet *he never swims*. As with so many lives, the really enjoyable activity is missed because the central character, economic man, is distracted by the sun-lounger or his drink or the shadow. But most importantly, he is enjoying not being at work *because he does not like his work*. His holiday represents an escape from his life, which is made unpleasant because of work he undertakes from pressure rather than from choice.

Marx was merely one of many economists who consider that work is an essential part of who we are as human beings, and that it is only work as it is structured within capitalism that is essentially unsatisfying - when it takes the form of a thin relationship between employee and employed, where power and physical or mental exertion, and increasingly skill and autonomy too, are swapped for money. While it is not a new idea that work is essential to who we are as members of a social species, it does seem to have slipped policy-makers' minds that if the workplace is dissatisfying - particularly if we spend an increasing proportion of our lives there - we will be dissatisfied human beings. This dissatisfaction will show itself in a variety of different ways, ranging from anti-social behaviour and drunkenness to an epidemic of drug-taking.

I am not the only commentator to have noticed that the disappearance of the full-time homemaker is an indication that more work is being extracted from each household. True, we do now have the benefit of more gadgets around our homes to replace her, and the general quality of those homes has probably increased, but is this sufficient substitute for the fact that it now requires two incomes to maintain a household, when a few decades ago only one was sufficient? From a Labour perspective this is a cause of celebration: more jobs than ever, more work than ever, more labour than ever. From a Marxist perspective it is unsurprising given the record profits being made by corporations. With the level of surplus value that is being extracted, of course we are having to run faster to keep the treadmill turning. From a human perspective, life has become ever more stressful and less satisfying. It seems fairly clear that as non-productive shareholders remove a larger slice of the economic pie, those of us who do work and produce will have to work ever harder to maintain our standing. The reason so many workers feel they are running faster and faster just to stand still is that they are dragging a whole bunch of increasingly greedy shareholders along with them.

The often touted solution to the problem of the work-life balance is to increase the provision of childcare. Rather than questioning why there is a trend towards more paid work outside the home, we find somebody to take the strain of our domestic work to enable us to continue our commitment to the capitalist economy. This person is probably a woman, and almost certainly poorly paid. The creation of her work, along with ours, increases GDP growth, and helps the Chancellor meet his targets, but does nothing for our quality of life. The same can be said of the proliferation of labour-saving devices and products, from tumble-dryers to TV dinners: where once we provided for ourselves now the market provides, with a corresponding loss to our self-sufficiency, our self-respect, and the planet, whose resources are used in the production of what we used to do for ourselves. This is not to suggest a return to the old model of a division of labour between a male breadwinner and a female homemaker. It is an argument more generally for a reduction in the hours in paid work spent by all members of a household.

For the working parent, especially the mother, the consequence of this childcare strategy is guilt and an increase in total working hours, as she crams quality time with children and domestic chores into the sliver of life between the end of work and the beginning of sleep. For some parents there may be feelings of guilt in leaving children in the care of others, particularly in cases where the available child care provision is not of a high enough standard. One solution for this may be to change the nature of the child care relationship, as discussed in the section on cooperatives below.

What is the consequence for children of this system of substituting market provided labour and commodities for time spent on producing goods and working within the household? Jamie Oliver has recently drawn attention to the abysmal way we are nourishing our children's bodies, but this is only one part of the epidemic of dis-ease amongst our children and young people. Their mental health seems even more precarious. In 2003 140,000 children between the ages of 16 and 18 in full-time education had been prescribed an anti-depressant. Since 1996 the number of young people under 16 being given Prozac and the related SSRIs has risen from 76,000 to 110,000. Ritalin prescriptions have rocketed from 92,000 in 1997 to 254,000 in 2002, a 326 per cent increase in just six years (see M. Townsend, *Observer*, 6.6.04). There is no direct evidence linking these trends with the loss of time shared between parents and children, but these statistics are evidence in themselves of a frightening crisis amongst our young people - which is largely being ignored. Other evidence suggests that a combination of loss of parental involvement because of longer working hours and an increase in certain types of TV viewing is leading to a rapid deterioration in our children's ability to speak.[5] 'Hard-working families' is a popular electoral slogan; its consequences may be less engaging.

So here are the problems we need to address: a poor quality of life in the workplace, with loss of autonomy and skills, loss of security and loss of self-esteem, together with increasing hours of work, means that, while home life is valued, its quality is also declining, with little time or energy left to maintain vital human relationships. This discussion about work and life, and where the distinction should be drawn, has lain at the heart of green political economy from the outset and has a central influence on green politics. I will attempt to share some of its insights in the limited space available here.[6]

Social and environmental sustainability

There are two concepts from green economics that have something to offer the project of rethinking the workplace in the twenty-first century: 'right livelihood' and 'self-provisioning'. If the central problem with capitalist expropriation is the increasing distance between producer and consumer, an obvious solution is to provide for your needs closer to home, ideally by your own hand. Once we reach the stage where you are providing yourself with the necessities of life we have achieved the self-sufficient ideal of self-provisioning.

---

5. National Literacy Trust is running a 'Talk to Your Baby' campaign, which specifically identifies increased working hours by parents as a cause of poor communication skills amongst children. The evidence on the issue of TV viewing is more mixed - see R. Close, *Television and language development in the early years: a review of the literature*, Literacy Trust 2004).

6. For further discussion, see E.F. Schumacher, *Good Work*, Cape 1979; J. Robertson, *Future Work: Jobs, Self-Employment and Leisure after the Industrial Age*, Gower 1985; M. Scott Cato, T. Keenoy, L. Arthur and R. Smith, 'Green and Red: An Exploration of the Cooperative Environmental Niche in Wales', paper for the Mondragon conference, June 2005; see also Andrea Westall in this issue.

No intervention by market middlemen, no excessive production of CO_2 in pointless transportation of goods, no unnecessary dependence on complex distribution systems. This might seem like a voluntaristic and individualist approach, but in fact the Green Party's economic policies, especially those concerned with trade, would facilitate such a shift. The defining characteristic of a sustainable trading system would be 'trade subsidiarity' - seeking supplies of each individual good or service as close to home as possible. Policies to support such a principle would include the introduction of a tax to reflect the environmental cost of transporting goods, and site-here-to-sell-here policies, as well as the establishment of a General Agreement on Sustainable Trade to support fair trade initiatives.

In terms of self-provisioning at the personal level, a good starting point is brushing up your cooking skills rather than relying on supermarket ready-meals. As well as withdrawing your money from the globalised market system, making your own food has the added advantage of being satisfying and better for your health. You can extend this thinking into the sphere of home improvements. Since it is your involvement in the global market that is the problem, employing local tradesmen or using your local LETS scheme or furniture recycling centre whenever you can is a step in the right direction. Extending this thinking further you might think about employing a local craftsman carpenter to build you a shelf-unit rather than bringing a flat-pack back from MFI in the back of your car. This will keep more value in your local economy and support skilled, self-employed, and probably more satisfied, workers. In terms of food production you might think about getting your hands dirty on your own allotment, or involving yourself in a box scheme, checking that as much of the produce in the box as possible is as local as possible.

Schumacher developed the concept of 'right livelihood' - one of the requirements of the Noble Eightfold Path of Buddhist teaching - to explain how our attitude to work might be in a green society. It defines a threefold purpose of work: to utilise and develop the faculties; to overcome our egocentric tendency by joining in a common task; and to produce goods and services that contribute to a 'becoming existence'. Clearly this might seem rather arcane for people working in a call-centre or ice-cream factory, but it can be helpful when making decisions about the sorts of directions our career paths might move as individuals, as well as guiding our policy-making to facilitate an economy that generates meaningful rather than soul-destroying employment. It would also suggest the need for the chance to pull back from the workplace and consider the direction one's life is taking, a process that would be supported by the introduction of a Citizens' Income scheme that allowed periodic breaks from the work treadmill.

Beyond these guiding concepts we must immediately acknowledge the most important principle in restructuring the economy: ownership matters. The cooperative structure offers an answer to the problem of ownership

'the most important principle in restructuring the economy is that ownership matters'

identified above. Research into the cooperative sector in Wales has shown that many co-operatives have been created as a defensive response to globalisation, as when international groups close parts of their businesses which are not making such large profits as other sections, although the business is valid and profitable in its own right. One example of this is Datrys Consulting, which was a successful branch of a Dutch-owned firm of consulting engineers that learned of its demise as part of a company restructuring plan. With the support of the Wales Cooperative Centre, the employees bought the Caernarfon-based company as a going concern from the Dutch parent, and they began trading as a cooperative in October 2002. The workforce continue to provide bilingual civil engineering services, maintaining five well-paid and highly skilled jobs in a depressed rural economy, and subsequently increasing them to eight.

I n the Welsh context, colleagues at the Wales Institute for Research into Cooperatives have also argued the advantage of cooperatives in terms of their ability to maintain value in the local economy, in contrast to the footloose nature of the global corporation. Worker-owners have actually bought their own job, so that as well as the value they generate through staying in the local economy, the job also has to stay. This is a process we have called 'capital anchoring', and it is particularly relevant against the backdrop of the vast sums wasted in Wales on paying East Asian corporations to bring in low-skilled low-paid jobs that lasted only a few years, whose main legacy was further demoralisation of the labour-force (for more details see www.uwic.ac.uk/ubs/research/wirc).

In contrast to the increasingly diffuse and insecure employment relationships generated by globalisation, Tower Colliery, the only employee-owned mine in the world and the last deep mine in South Wales, is a positive and life-affirming workplace. Employment and environmental standards are high, there is a strong sense of camaraderie, and decisions about how much of the surplus from sales should be reinvested in the business or paid as bonuses are made by democratic meetings. On a smaller scale, Sundance Renewables, a worker cooperative in the Amman Valley, has created five jobs in the growing renewable energy sector, including one as an apprentice. The business operates the country's first cooperative biodiesel recycling plant.

Cooperatives have also been proposed as a solution to the inadequacy of provision of childcare. A mutual solution in this market would offer many of the advantages offered by cooperatives wherever they operate. One might think particularly of the retention by local economies, often deprived local economies, of the full value of the work of local people, and of the increased participation in a richer relationship than the thin market relationship, an aspect which may be particularly important to parents when it comes to care of their children. The cooperative can balance the needs of children, parents and employees, creating a full, trusting relationship that can fulfil all their needs.

Research by Dunance and colleagues found that mothers are far more concerned about a whole range of hands-on issues about the kind of care their children receive than is generally acknowledged in national policies.[7] The cooperative model, with parents owning and being closely involved in the management of the nursery where their children spend time, is likely to allow them the flexibility they want to create a childcare setting that suits their needs. The data demonstrate that this model for childcare is by no means marginal. The cooperative model for childcare provision represents around two-thirds of the overall provision (i.e. cooperatives owned either by parents or by employees[8]).

The green response to apparently intractable policy problems is often one of withdrawal and voluntarism. With Gandhi, I see this as a positive and empowered move, but such a response fails to take account of people's different

---

7. S. Dunance et al, 'Mothers and Child Care: Policies, Values and Theories', *Children & Society*, 18/4, 2004.
8. Cooperatives-UK, *Delivering Cooperative Childcare: Briefing Document*, 2004.

inheritances of social and educational capital, and their different levels of spiritual development. It may appear to be a contradiction in terms to suggest macro-level policies to encourage developments which are inherently locally based. But there are ways in which the policy framework could facilitate diverse local economic responses, and perhaps especially constrain the crushing power of the market in all areas of life. The Citizens' Income scheme, building confidence in economic security and allowing creativity to flourish, is an obvious first step. Beyond that, we need to challenge the state aid rules of the European Union, which prevent even the smallest sums of money being made available as grants to develop local enterprises. Not content with leveraging money out of local economies, corporations have also lobbied to make it impossible to invest public money in non-public-sector enterprises, even when these are unquestionably in the public interest. Policies to reinternalise the externalities created by the global trading system, primarily the introduction of a carbon tax, would instantly change the relative prices of locally produced versus globally traded goods, enabling the expansion of self-provisioning.

And how are we to deal with the long-hours culture? I would suggest the most important response is to readjust our judgement about what is important and what brings us happiness in life, a judgement which has been distorted by the need on the part of the market and its advertising industry to create unfulfilled desires for goods and services. The market system thrives on the 'ethic of scarcity', encouraging us to see the glass as half empty to encourage us back onto the treadmill. We are more dissatisfied than our primitive ancestors, whose societies have been called the original affluent societies, and whose approach to production and exchange has been described in terms of 'stone age economics':

There are two possible courses to affluence. Wants may be 'easily satisfied' either by producing much or desiring little. The familiar conception, the Galbraithean way, makes assumptions peculiarly appropriate to market economies: that man's wants are great, not to say infinite, whereas his means are limited, although improvable: thus, the gap between means and ends can be narrowed by industrial productivity, at least to the point that 'urgent goods' become plentiful. But there is also a Zen road to affluence, departing from premises somewhat different from our own: that human material wants are finite and few, and technical means unchanging but on the whole adequate. Adopting the Zen strategy, a people can enjoy an unparalleled material plenty - with a low standard of living.[9]

This conclusion is based on ethnographic observation of hunter-gatherer societies, whose people are always well provided with food and who spend far more time in group activities which we might characterise as leisure-based or cultural than members of industrialised societies, and far less in work. Thus a group of native Australians from Fish Creek spent an average of five hours per day gathering and preparing food (their work), while the Hadza of Tanzania, who have not been pushed into more marginal land, spent less than two hours per day on average on this activity.

Pre-capitalist employment systems have much to recommend them and were hotly defended during the rise of the wage-labour system, as described in *The Making of the English Working Class*.[10] In spite of our preconception that life was 'nasty brutish and short' in the middle ages, we find that days were defined not by the absence of work, as we define with our 'bank holidays', but rather by the absence of a religious festival, the *dies non festivus*, which was a day when you unfortunately had to work. Thompson describes the difficulty the early capitalists found in organising their workforces to obey the clock and to abandon Saint Monday, the day spent recovering from the excesses of the weekend rather than working.

Of course I am not suggesting a return to either of these types of life: with our vastly increased technical ability and scientific knowledge we could ensure for ourselves a much higher standard of living with far less work effort expended and with far less pressure on the planet. To achieve this we need to change our attitudes as individuals. We need to reappraise what we really value, as distinct from what has a market or monetary value. We need to learn to live within the ethic of plenty and with a sense of gratitude for the planet that provides us with that plenty. And finally, we need to reject the competitive ethos of capitalism with its undermining of the relationships of trust that have always made human societies what they are. Creating cooperative workplaces and rebuilding the mutualist approach to solving social problems are important parts of that process.

---

9. M. Sahlins, *Stone Age Economics*, Aldine Altherton 1972, p2.
10. E.P. Thompson, *The Making of the English Working Class*, Gollancz, 1963.

The architecture of social democracy

Ken Worpole

Ken Worpole *looks at ways in which architecture and design could contribute to a humanisation of our cities.*

All buildings speak: some more directly than others. If you sit on the top deck of any bus travelling down the busy Walworth Road in south London, you will pass a building on which a plaque is mounted at first floor level, inscribed in bas-relief, 'The Health of the People is the Highest Law'. The building, a former Public Health Department, was opened on 27 September 1937, at a time when the Metropolitan Borough of Southwark, under Labour Party control, was famous for its commitment to providing free parks, gardens, clinics, nursery schools and other public amenities to a largely working-class population, many of whom lived in conditions of serious poverty.

Close by, the Peckham Health Centre, designed by engineer Sir Owen Williams, was opened two years earlier, in 1935. Also known as the Pioneer Health Centre, it included a swimming pool, gymnasium, theatre, nursery, dance halls, a cafeteria and games rooms, as well as medical facilities.[1] It quickly

---

1. Today the Peckham Health Centre has been converted into private apartments, known as 'The Pioneer Building', with estate agents emphasising the building's 'active theme with a stunning indoor pool, a gym and outdoor tennis court.' (Property advertisement, *Independent on Sunday*, 9.1.05.) Thus are the public ideals of one generation turned into the speculative interests of another.

Plaque on wall of Public Health Department, 1937

became famous throughout the world as the most fully developed - and most architecturally inspiring - approach to public health care. When the eminent architect Walter Gropius arrived as a refugee in England in 1937 he declared it to be not only the best new building in London, but also the most interesting one. There was a distinction.

Between the Walworth Road building and the Peckham Health Centre you can still find the Brockwell Park Lido. This also opened in 1935 (one of more than twenty other lidos in London built in the same decade), and was designed by Harry Arnold Rowbothan and T.L. Smithson, both of whom worked in the London County Council Parks Department for much of their lives. This was an era in which municipal architects came into their own; they were responsible for much that was best in the public architecture of their time.

The period was an era of great political investment in public health, a pattern common across much of Europe. Health centres, clinics, lidos and nursery schools were amongst the most innovative new building types being developed, and modernist ideas and ideals were rapidly transplanted from one country to another. Berthold Lubetkin's Finsbury Health Centre, completed in 1938, was partly based on designs Lubetkin had originally done for a Palace of Soviets, and owed something to El Lissitsky's famous Red Wedge. On the large curving walls of the foyer, the designer Gordon Cullen had been commissioned to produce two murals, based on the slogans, 'Live out of doors as much as you can' and 'Fresh air night and day'. The murals have gone but the building itself still functions successfully, otherwise unchanged.

Many today would question the quasi-anthropological language then used to describe these progressive experiments in public health provision; and the technical prospectuses were often couched in the vocabulary of positivistic social engineering. A close look at the documentation which surrounded their planning, design and monitoring of effects suggests more than a hint of social and genetic determinism, of apprehensions about 'fitness to marry and breed' and of declining class vitalism. Nevertheless they represent a period in which progressive politics and modern architecture marched in step, and in the same direction.

This heroic age of socially committed public architecture is now generally overlooked, or simply forgotten. Yet the achievements of social democratic policies in Europe in the twentieth century are reflected as much in forms of town planning, architecture and landscape design as they are in forms of

Lubetkin's Finsbury Health Centre, 1938

organisational and economic development; and they have done more to shape the lives of people, for the good, than many other kinds of political intervention. Architectural historian Thomas A. Markus has observed the same tendency towards historical amnesia amongst historians of culture. 'Historians and art critics dealing with the creative arts have excluded architecture', he wrote. 'How is it that both the historians and the critics of art and society deny buildings the power to transform society?'[2]

This concern with the material culture of place is not just about buildings. As British landscape architect Sir Geoffrey Jellicoe wrote in the 1970s, in the twentieth century the collective landscape emerged as a 'social necessity'.[3] Then and now there has been much invaluable work in urban design, place-making, and public space culture (with as many failures as successes, admittedly), but it has too often been invisible to radical political groupings obsessed with economism and matters of political organisational form. Yet nowhere is political form more expressive than in buildings and constructed landscapes. For example, the linear park at Norr Malarstrand in Stockholm, designed by Erik Glemme in 1939 to create a green link between the city centre and the suburbs for pedestrians, cyclists and others, was decades ahead of its time, socially and environmentally. Three-quarters of a century later, his robust and elegant design remains a much loved feature of that beautiful city, a case study in visionary urban design that is now being emulated throughout the world.

In ignoring these great achievements in urban design and planning, progressive thinkers are in danger of ceding hard-fought territory to the avatars of economic liberalism and laisser-faire planning - including many in New Labour - who are happy to allow the market to allocate and distribute the spatial and institutional resources of the city. The architecture and landscape design inspired by the political aspirations of early twentieth-century social democracy remains a legacy worth celebrating. I sought to recover some of this history in my book *Here comes the sun: architecture and public space in twentieth century European culture* (Reaktion 2000). This was essentially a story

2. Thomas A. Markus, *Buildings and Power: Freedom and Control in the Origin of Modern Building Types*, London 1993, p26.
3. Geoffrey and Susan Jellicoe, *The Landscape of Man*, Thames & Hudson, London 1995.

Park Malarstrand

about how, at the beginning of the twentieth century, social reformers, planners and architects tried to re-make the city in the image of a sun-lit, ordered utopia. The astonishing growth in demand for new institutions and buildings in Europe in the early years of the twentieth century arose directly from the rise of democracy, particularly through the ideas and political institutions of the left. A newly enfranchised citizenry and its political organisations confidently demanded better housing, health, education, transport, public landscapes and even leisure facilities - and architects of the modern school energetically responded.

Modernism and socialism in alliance

For a while social democracy seemed to form a natural alliance with the pioneers of architectural modernism (of which a rather austere functionalism was an early begetter), though this was at least as much to do with their common universalising energies as it was with a shared set of ethical or cultural beliefs. Certainly the principal actors involved in both movements had little in common personally, one suspects. European social democratic politicians tended to have emerged from trade union or non-conformist religious backgrounds and left-wing social movements, whereas the architects were more likely to have come from well-educated, cosmopolitan bourgeois families, rich enough to afford the lengthy academic and technical training. While it lasted, however, the two forces together created a whirlwind that changed the face of towns and cities throughout Europe.

Parallel to these ideals was the social democratic mission to secure the health and well-being of the people from the cradle to the grave, signalled in the Southwark plaque mentioned at the beginning. This required the development of a whole new range of building types and institutions. The nursery school, the health centre, the sanatorium, the public library, the public housing estate, the open air school, the sports park, the lido, and even the cemetery, all became chosen commissions and projects for many of the early modernist architects.

The healthy growth and social development of children was an early rallying point for progressive politics. In Britain the Macmillan sisters established London's first School Clinic in 1908, and in 1914 they set up a permanent tented camp for sick children in the garden of Evelyn House in Deptford, another south London trail-blazer. (Where are the psycho-geographers when you really need them?) This was a pioneer of the fresh-air school movement in Britain and beyond: by 1937, there were 96 open-air day schools and 53 open-air residential schools in England alone. In Amsterdam, the famous Open-air School, designed by Johannes Duiker and Bernard Bijvoet, was completed in 1928, and architects flocked from around the world to see it. Built before Aalto's Paimio Sanatorium in Finland, this is one of the greatest early achievements of the new architecture predicated on health and sunshine. Nearly eighty years later, the school remains resolutely modern, a visual and structural delight, still bustling with life.

Another pioneering design in the field of progressive education was the 'School on the Sound' by architect Kaj Gottlob in Copenhagen, completed in 1938. This had an oval central hall or atrium reaching from floor to ceiling, with clerestory light entering at the top. The school was built on four floors, each with a balcony looking down into the main hall, on the floor of which was a large inlaid map of greater Copenhagen. The ceiling is decorated with a great compass rose, as befits a school within sight of the Baltic Sea.

The Dutch in particular were great pioneers of high quality public housing, recruiting the best and most visionary architects. The 'Amsterdam School' of architecture, perhaps the most consistently innovative and successful architectural 'school' of the twentieth century, achieved its international reputation working for radical and religious housing associations for tenants on low incomes. The Eigen Haard (Our Hearth) estate designed by Michael De Klerk and completed in 1920, along with De Dageraad (The Dawn) by De Klerk and P.L. Kramer, completed in 1922, both in Amsterdam, are well worth a detour when visiting the city, and still astonish by the quality of the design, materials and the sheer exuberant detailing of the interiors and facades.

In and near Rotterdam, the city architect J.J.P. Oud (1890-1963) designed two of the most exquisite housing estates ever, the Hook of Holland estate, constructed between 1924 and 1927, and the Kiekhof Estate in Rotterdam, completed in 1929. The long narrow window line which runs along the top of the Kiekhof terrace is distinctively Dutch, and both have recently been restored, employing the original De Stijl colour scheme. For a while Oud and the painter Piet Mondrian were close colleagues.

Oud's Hook of Holland Estate, 1924-7

Tait's Silver End Estate, 1926-32

In Britain a similar alliance between architecture and progressive housing policies resulted in the Silver End Estate in Essex. This was designed by Thomas Tait, also the architect of the inspiring German Hospital in Hackney, modelled partly on Aalto's Paimio Sanatorium, and one of the leading modernists of his time. The Essex estate was commissioned by Francis Crittall, the metal window manufacturer and radical philanthropist, and constructed between 1926 and 1932. Silver End was a utopian experiment in housing and living, built principally to house the Crittall factory workers, but homes were also provided for striking miners who could not go back to their original jobs. In its first decade it was cited as the healthiest settlement in England, and had the lowest death rate and the highest birth rate anywhere. The village had its own park, farm, hotel and village hall, and food was locally produced.

The postwar period
Much of this great legacy was overshadowed after the Second World War

by the notable failures of mass-production public architecture in the International Style, resulting from programmes of slum clearance and 'comprehensive re-development'. Up went vast housing estates and tower blocks, often devoid of amenities such as pubs and shops, and cut off from the social and economic networks of the city centres (including the informal economy). Cities were, symbolically and literally, re-configured to prioritise the needs of car traffic flows above all else: city centres were cut off from their residential hinterlands by ring roads impassable to walkers, particularly those pushing prams or laden with shopping. New hospitals, town halls, and other public service buildings were designed as fortresses surrounded by vast moats of car-parking space. The scale at which human activity best flourished - especially walking - was replaced by a scale of monumentalist planning most convenient to regional traffic policies.[4] Economies of scale and macro-planning triumphed over economies of localism and elements of self-management.

Now that era is also coming to an end, as attempts are made to rein in the destructive effects of the car on urban life and vitality, and to recreate 'liveable communities' where it is hoped that more people will learn to play a greater part in designing and managing their own environment. The renewed political interest by New Labour in the politics of place (notably through a concern for street design and street quality) is welcome, though at present it seems to grow more out of a politics of social control than deeply held aspirations for individual and collective flourishing.[5]

A number of the newer think-tanks have also been busy 'rethinking' a range of key public buildings and institutions. Staff at Demos have worked with those at the Architectural Foundation in London (and latterly the Design Council) to rethink the design of the school, the hospital and the prison, whilst the

---

4. I dealt with some of these trends in *Towns for People*, Open University Press, 1992.
5. The list of first and second term New Labour government reports and action plans on re-building communities and place-based environmental renewal programmes is becoming inordinately long, a worrying sign in itself of too many documents replacing too little action on the ground. Nevertheless the creation of CABE (Commission for Architecture and the Built Environment) out of the ashes of the former Royal Fine Art Commission and, within CABE, the development of the even newer CABE SPACE, are proving to be a power for the good. Two reports of particular significance are 'Green Spaces, Better Places: Final Report of the Urban Green Spaces Task Force' (2002), and 'Living Places: Caring for Quality' (2004).

Institute of Public Policy Research has been busy rethinking the town hall and the police station. Not surprisingly, architects have been heavily involved in these discussions, increasingly through the offices of CABE (Commission for Architecture and the Built Environment). This is happening at 'a time when Britain faces the biggest period of public building since the 1960s', according to *Prospect* (No 106, January 2005). Capital budgets for public buildings rose from £19.2bn in 2000-01 to £32.4bn in 2003-04. In addition various Lottery funds have supported a whole new generation of arts centres, community centres, museums, galleries and park refurbishments (including new buildings).

Yet there is no architectural common style any more, let alone a shared political vision for a new architectural philosophy - other than an often tokenistic concession to energy-saving. There are a lot of 'signature' or 'icon' buildings, beloved of architects and commissioning politicians in a hurry to make their name, but most lack any real iterative power. Corporate office buildings are today amongst the most prestigious architectural commissions, along with sports stadiums, international convention centres, airports, art galleries, museums and civil engineering projects such as bridges and major road schemes. The fine grain architecture and urban design needed to humanise the town or the city is no longer of interest to the big names. Sir Norman Foster's Swiss:Re development in London (aka 'The Gherkin'), whilst winning the RIBA Stirling Prize in 2004, is nevertheless rightly criticised for sterilising the public area around it, adding nothing to the life of the city in which this engineering marvel is set.

Not all is bad, though. Other short-listed projects for the 2004 Stirling Prize included the beautiful Hoyle Early Years Centre at Bury in Lancashire, designed by DSDHA, Maggie's Cancer Caring Respite Centre in Dundee designed by Frank Gehry with James T. Stephen, and the Berners Pool, a community swimming pool at Grange over Sands, designed by Hodder Associates (who elsewhere blotted their copybook with the disastrous Clissold Leisure Centre in Hackney).

There is also renewed architectural interest in designing public libraries. Thanks to the revival of the fortunes of the public library - largely as a result of the Internet - there have been some high profile and exciting new library buildings appearing around the country, in which a genuine commitment to public domain democracy can at least be discerned.

Volume house-building, however, remains resolutely untouched by any new thinking about changing demographic and social patterns, design, materials, or environmental impact. There is nothing remotely to compare to the pioneering idea of communal land ownership which inspired Letchworth Garden City, which even today allows the Letchworth Garden City Heritage Foundation to capture and distribute all increases in land value in the form of local amenities such as a day hospital, grants to schools and arts facilities. What innovation there is results from the work of a very small number of housing associations, such as The Peabody Trust.

There have been some positive developments in the design of new school buildings or the 'retro-fitting' of existing ones (notably in the successful collaboration between School Works, Demos, the Architecture Foundation and Southwark Council at Kingsdale School in Dulwich, south London, along with architects de Rijke Marsh Morgan), but the bane of much new public building is the notorious Public Finance Initiative (PFI) scheme. This is designed to transfer the risk of building and maintaining new schools, hospitals, prisons and other public sector institutions to private capital. To a degree it does this, but it does so at the expense of asset-stripping and de-skilling local authorities in their historic role as architects, planners and publicly accountable asset-holders. At the same time, PFI projects tend to produce bland, 'design-and-build' formulaic architecture that pays little or no attention to local circumstances or conditions. Between 1998 and 2003, 240 schools, 34 hospitals and 23 transport projects have been developed using PFI schemes, and few if any have raised a flicker of architectural interest or a quickening of the public pulse in terms of local pride or delight.

A return to the political and cultural conditions which produced the politics of mass social democracy at the beginning of the twentieth century is, of course, impossible, as would be a return to the welfare paternalism which informed much of its institutional culture. Nevertheless there is today another opportunity to create a public debate around the issue of the social responsibilities of architects, landscape designers and planners, and there now are a number of bodies now rising to this challenge - such as CABE,

Demos, the Design Council, IPPR, and even the Heritage Lottery Fund (which has funded a number of new buildings or extensions to or in museums, libraries and public parks). Yet on these matters, the left has to date remained largely silent.

All photographs taken by Larraine Worpole

This essay develops some of the ideas presented originally as a photographic slide-show about twentieth century European social architecture at the international conference on 'Re-thinking Social Democracy' held in London in April 2004.

Climate change

A case study from Kazakhstan

Stephan Harrison

Stephan Harrison *argues that changes in glaciers, arising from climate change, pose increasingly serious environmental and political problems for those living in their vicinity.*

Climate change has some obvious consequences which have captured the imagination. We see pictures of the flooding in Europe during the summer of 2002, followed by the heatwaves of 2003 which killed at least 20,000 people in western and southern Europe. We are reminded of the reality of sea level rise caused by the thermal expansion of sea water and the melting of mountain ice caps, and the effects that this is having on the low-lying islands of the Pacific. Yet climate change has the potential to affect human society in more subtle ways; by destabilising economies and upsetting political and social relationships, it will play an important role in creating the context within which countries develop and relate to their neighbours and the wider international community. It is the purpose of this article to examine some of these issues by focusing on the evidence for recent climate change, and its likely future effects, in central Asia.

The science of climate change is well established. In 1990 the Intergovernmental Panel on Climate Change (IPCC) First Assessment Report synthesised the clear scientific consensus on the nature and direction of contemporary climate change, but was unable to attribute an unequivocal human contribution to this. By the Second Assessment Report of 1995, it was recognised that there was a discernible human influence on the global climate.

From the perspective of the early twenty-first century we can now see that the 1990s was the warmest decade in the instrumental record, and that the three hottest years on record have been 1998, 2002 and 2003.

 Since the 1970s in the UK, the incidence of above-average wet months has more than doubled, and the number of unusually hot months has gone up by 50 per cent. The European heatwave of 2003 is now very likely to have been significantly reinforced by society's greenhouse gas emissions,[1] and recently we have learnt that global atmospheric concentrations of carbon dioxide increased by over 2ppm in 2002 and 2003, in the absence of an obvious trigger. This is causing considerable concern amongst climatologists since it may reflect the operation of feedback processes which are not yet fully accounted for in our computer models.

One of the anticipated outcomes of this global warming is the reduction of mountain ice cover and permafrost, and this is underway in almost all mountain regions. In much of central Asia, these glaciers and ice-rich permafrost behave as water towers, by providing a continuous supply of fresh water to the lowlands and thereby allowing economic activity to take place. Their recession over the past few decades in response to global climate change is striking, and this is well seen in the mountains of the northern Tien Shan in Kazakhstan. Here glacier retreat affects the nature of the natural hazards in the populated valleys and the lowland piedmont zone and, more widely, has potential geopolitical implications.

Mountain regions fringing the arid zones of Central Asia are facing increasing demand for water resources and tourism-leisure activities. These pressures are particularly acute in Kazakhstan which is, apart from Russia, the largest of the former Soviet Republics. Kazakhstan has huge reserves of fossil fuels and other mineral deposits, is a large agricultural producer, and has developed an industrial sector based upon the extraction and processing of these natural resources. The early years following the breakup of the USSR in 1991 were a time of economic contraction in Kazakhstan. However, by 1995-97 a programme of economic reform and privatisation moved many assets into the private sector. Between 2000 and 2002 the economy grew at around 10

---

1. See, for example, P.A. Stott, D.A. Stone and M.R. Allen, 'Human contribution to the European heatwave of 2003', *Nature* 432, 2004.

per cent per year, although there has been a significant widening of the gap between rich and poor. Since independence, there has also been a sharp decline in the organisation of energy, environmental and resource planning between the central Asian republics, and this is likely to have unforeseen economic and environmental consequences.

Figure 1. Location maps showing Kazakhstan and the Bolshaya and Malaya Almatinka valleys.

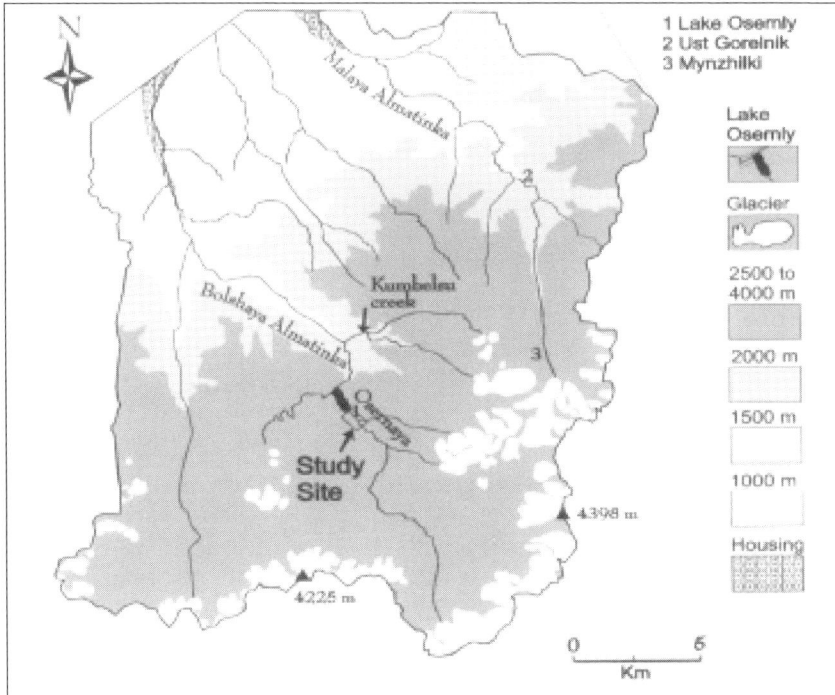

The study site where mudflows are particularly well developed is shown above

Figure 2. The city of Almaty lying at the foot of the Tien Shan mountains.

The city and hinterland of Almaty, located in the highly populated piedmont zone of the Zailiisky Alatau mountains, in the northern Tien Shan of Kazakhstan, forms the economic powerhouse of the country (Figures 1 and 2). This region is the focus for 20 per cent of the country's industrial production and 30 per cent of its agricultural production, and hosts 17 per cent of its population. The area draws its water supply principally from two sources. The first is from the transboundary Ili River, which rises in the mountains of northwest China and flows westwards into southern Kazakhstan, and fills the Kapchagay Reservoir and Lake Balkash to the north of Almaty. The second, and only local and reliable supply of water for the city, comes from the glaciated Bolshaya and Malaya Almatinka drainage basins lying 30km south of Almaty. These valleys are also the focus of an expanding tourism and leisure-based economy that is reflected in the establishment since the 1970s of several large sports complexes and numerous holiday homes and resorts.

However, like many glaciated mountain regions, these valleys are prone to experience severe flooding, avalanches and catastrophic debris flows that disrupt transport and utility infrastructure and endanger human activity. The frequency and magnitude of such hazardous processes has prompted a long history of climatological and geomorphological monitoring in the study area, by the International Centre of Geoecology of the Mountain Countries in Arid Regions (ICGM, based in the Institute of Geography), and the Institute of Permafrost, Russian Academy of Sciences. The ICGM maintains two mountain research stations in these valleys, which have been instrumental in maintaining unusually long and detailed records of recent historic environmental change. These records include late nineteenth and twentieth century glacier fluctuations (for example, moraines of the Tuyuksu glacier have been dated using historical records dating back to 1923); a wide range of climate parameters (collected daily since 1879 at the mountain station in the Malaya Almatinka valley); and the frequency and character of avalanche and rock glacier activity over the past forty years.[2]

From this data set, it is clear that climate change is having an impact in

2. H. Schröder, A. Kokarev and S. Harrison, 'Rock glaciers in the northern Tien Shan, Kazakhstan: new data on movement rates and distribution', *Glacial Geology and Geomorphology*.

the region, and this is evident from an analysis of the meteorological data and the response of mountain glaciers.

Changes in air temperature

Mean annual air temperatures from 1936 to 1998 show a rise in air temperatures from the 1980s which are now about 0.2–0.25°C above the long term trend. In the mountains mean annual air temperatures from the Bolshaya Almatinskoye Lake show a 0.8°C rise over this period, slightly higher than the 0.6°C rise in Global Mean Surface Temperatures over the past century reported in the 2001 IPCC report.

Seasonal variations in the northern Tien Shan are also apparent. Mean January temperatures in Almaty have increased (but remain below zero). Whilst fluctuations of mean January temperatures recorded at the mountain stations are within the limits of natural variability, these values were at their highest for over 100 years during the 1990s. Mean air temperatures in November and December (months when continuous snow cover at low and mid-altitudes develops) have increased significantly (between 2 and 3°C) between 1936 and 1998.

Glaciers and climate change

The glaciers of the region occur in four main locations: the Tekes, Charyn and Ili River basins which lie to the east of Almaty and those of the Zailiiskiy Alatau range of the Tien Shan to the south of Almaty (see Figure 1). The glaciers are mainly small valley and cirque glaciers located in the remote upper reaches of the high valleys. Their small size makes them very responsive to changing climatic conditions, which means that their response times are in the order of a year or two. The frontal positions of these glaciers have been monitored by analysis of repeat aerial photographs since the 1940s and from this it is clear that they have been in recession over the past few decades. As a result of their short response times, we can be certain that these glaciers are responding to recent climate changes, and that their behaviour is not a delayed response to the warming at the end of the Little Ice Age in the late nineteenth century.

In the mountains of the northern Tien Shan 416 glaciers have been monitored over the last fifty years or so and it is also clear that they are melting very rapidly; losing about 0.7 per cent of their mass per year between 1955-2000.[3] In consequence, the glaciers reduced their total surface area over this time from 272 km^2 to 201 km^2. One glacier stands out. Observations on the Tuyuksu glacier, some 30 km south of Almaty, have been carried out by Kazakh scientists since early in the last century, making it one of the most closely studied glaciers in the world. This gives us an excellent opportunity to examine the response of glaciers to climate change.

The Tuyuksu Glacier

The Tuyuksu glacier is a small valley glacier some 5 km in length and 4 km^2 in area. It was first studied in detail in 1902 but certain measurements on the glacier date back to the 1870s, making these one of the longest continuous glaciological data sets in the world, and of considerable interest to glacial modellers and climatologists. Further detailed investigations (such as research monitoring ice thickness) were started during the International Geophysical Year between 1957 and 1959, with additional hydrological studies being carried out from 1965.

Mass balance data describes the balance between inputs to the glacier system (mainly in the form of snowfall and ice from avalanches into the accumulation zone) and outputs (mainly as a result of melting in the ablation zone). Whether the mass balance of a glacier is positive or negative therefore defines its 'health' and allows us to describe quantitatively whether the glacier is gaining or losing mass. For the Tuyuksu Glacier, the mass balance data we have so far are from 1879-2001. Mass balance was mostly positive between the end of the nineteenth century to the first two decades of the twentieth century. However, from the middle of the twentieth century there was a shift to mostly negative mass balances, and this has continued into this century. This pattern is typical for most of the glaciers in the area (and most similar sized mountain glaciers elsewhere on earth). Only the smaller glaciers at high altitudes in the Tien Shan (above 3650m) are currently experiencing positive mass balances. Since there appears to be a strong positive correlation between mass balance and the height of the regional snow line and large-scale atmospheric circulation patterns, the

3. H. Schroeder and I. Severskiy (eds), *Water Resources in the basin of the Ili River (Republic of Kazakhstan)*, Mensch and Buch Verlag 2004.

Tuyuksu glacier is predicted to have positive mass balance when the annual precipitation is greater than 1240mm rain equivalent, or when the total ablation is less than about 1080mm water equivalent.

Internal mass exchange through the glacier system occurs through a combination of accumulation, ablation and glacier dynamics. Every year, some 0.8-2.0 million tonnes of ice are transferred by glacier flow from the accumulation to the ablation zone. This, however, is insufficient to compensate for total ablation and therefore the glacier has a strongly negative mass balance at the present time. Between 1923 and 1957, the terminus of the Tuyuksu glacier receded some 360m up valley and its area reduced by 95000m². From 1957 to 1984, the glacier retreated a further 380m. This represents a loss of about 12 per cent in volume. The recession of the Tuyuksu glacier continues at the present time (Figure 3). The snout retreated 9.2m between 1997 and 1998, 10.7m between 1998 and 1999, and a further 10m in 2000. The last measurements we have (for 2001) show that the glacier has a strongly negative mass balance (-700 mm water equivalent), and this continues the trend of the last 24 years, during which the mass balance has been positive only once, in 1993.

Whilst these responses of glaciers are clearly of interest to scientists, they also warn of profound changes which may affect the livelihoods of millions of people in central Asia. Many of the rivers which supply irrigation schemes in the area are fed by glaciers and permafrost in the high mountains. More than 90 per cent of the region's water supplies are used for irrigation and most of the central Asian states are increasing the amount of land under irrigation. In southern Kazakhstan, much of this water is stored in two areas: Lake Balkash and the Kapchagay Reservoir. Lake Balkash covers over 18,000 km² and is one of the largest inland lakes of central Asia. However, it is becoming increasingly saline; a result of increased evaporation and decreased inflow from the Ili River, such that its eastern arm has salinity levels above 4g/l, which means that the water is now largely unsuitable for both irrigation and drinking.

Since 75-80 per cent of river runoff in the region is derived from glaciers and permafrost, with glacier recession the water supply is threatened, and with it the farming economy. Water supply problems also have the potential to destabilise the political situation in the region, since many of the rivers are transboundary; glaciers in one state feed rivers supplying water in another. For instance, China has produced plans to abstract water from the Ili River to develop its industrial capacity in Xinjiang province. Despite the recent signing of intergovernmental agreements between Kazakhstan and China covering the protection of transboundary rivers (such as that signed in Astana in September 2001), it is clear that China's plans to abstract up to 40 per cent of the water from the Irtysh and Ili River basins will exacerbate the water supply problems to both Lake Balkash and the Kapshagay Reservoir.

Sustainable water resource use cannot therefore be achieved without a high level of political agreement and there remains the threat of conflicts developing over water supply.

Not only has this increasing threat of aridity the potential to negatively affect economic activity in the piedmont zone, glacier recession has also created two main natural hazards which threaten the southern suburbs of Almaty. First, the retreat of glaciers has uncovered huge amounts of unconsolidated glacial debris which now chokes tributary and main valleys. During periods of heavy rain, these are remobilised and form destructive debris flows which travel rapidly downvalley into the southern suburbs of Almaty. The majority of regional debris flow events (c.70 per cent) are triggered by

Figure 3. Small glaciers of the northern Tien Shan mountains at about 3000m altitude.

Figure 4. Looking downstream of the moraine deposited by the Tuyuksu glacier in the 19th century. Unvegetated debris from the 1973 flood covers much of the valley floor.

intense precipitation associated with the penetration of cold wet air masses from the north-west.

More dangerously, recent glacier retreat has lead to the development of moraine dammed glacial lakes. Since the moraine dam is frequently unstable, these lakes periodically drain catastrophically, and the subsequent debris flows pose a significant natural hazard to the city. One of the most powerful recent debris flows to affect the northern valleys of the Tien Shan occurred in July 1973 in the Malaya Almatinka valley. The flow was caused by the breaching of a moraine-dammed lake at an altitude of 3400m, which had developed because of the twentieth century recession of the Tuyuksu glacier. From 1963 to 1973 the lake had more than tripled in volume, and by 1973 the lake was 380m long, 142m wide and up to 13.6m deep, and contained over 250,000 cubic metres of water. In the late afternoon of 15 July 1973 the moraine dam finally failed, creating a huge lake outburst flood. The water quickly picked up sediment from the moraine and the valley sides and travelled rapidly down valley. By the time the resulting debris flow reached Mynzhilki, some 2km downstream and at an altitude of 3010 m, the flow was travelling at about 4m per second and maximum discharge was some 280 cubic metres per second. This caused the valley floor to be incised to a depth of 10-15m in a few minutes at a number of locations. Less than 30 minutes after the initial moraine dam failure the mixture of water and debris had reached the large dam and storage reservoir above Almaty, into which 4 million cubic metres of debris was deposited.

Large sums of money are diverted to pay for engineering solutions to these hazards and these represent a significant additional economic cost from climate change.

What is now required from this region is a greater understanding of the magnitude, frequency and controls of landscape-forming events such as these floods, and information relating to the spatial and temporal pattern of potentially hazardous geomorphic activity under varied climate and land-use changes. From this, we may be able to develop management frameworks for water resource and tourism/leisure activities that are both realistic and sustainable.

Figure 5. Incised reach of the Malaya Almatinka valley. The prominent line of boulders to the left of the stream was deposited in the 1973 flood.

Wider implications

More generally, the recent behaviour of glaciers and other ice bodies also provides a compelling argument against the small, but vociferous, group of climate change sceptics who argue that there is no evidence for global warming. Their position hinges on a number of points, but their main issue concerns the validity of the temperature record. They argue that the instrumental record of climate change is contaminated by urban heat island effects, and reason that the recent steep rise of land temperatures identified globally can be explained by the fact that many meteorological stations are situated in or near urban areas. For instance, the longest instrumental record of climate is the central England temperature record which stretches back in one form to 1659, but the sceptics argue that this records the increased urbanisation of central England since this time, rather than any synoptic scale climate change. Despite the best efforts of climate modellers and climatologists to show that they have accounted for urbanisation in their analyses of the data, the sceptics have used this uncertainty effectively to cast doubt on the validity of the entire climate change programme. As a result, the evidence of climate change at a global scale from small remote glaciers is invaluable, as these records cannot have been contaminated by urban heat islands. Since the vast majority of glaciers in this region of central Asia have negative mass balances, we can be confident that there is strong evidence for contemporary climate change in this region.

Conclusions

The case of Kazakhstan shows how intimately related are climate, landscape, and political and economic systems, and that assessing the risks from future climate change is not just a question of producing flood hazard maps or knowing where sea level rises will affect coastlines. A similar analysis to that presented here, and yielding similar results, could be conducted in many regions of the world. For example, in the Indian and Nepal Himalaya and in Peru, glacier retreat has produced a number of unstable moraine-dammed lakes which threaten the lives of thousands of people living downvalley of them. Glacier retreat and permafrost melting in the European Alps is affecting hydro-electric power schemes and reducing the stability of cable car stations and other infrastructure in the high valleys. In Patagonia, the dramatic retreat of the San Rafael Glacier over the last decade will have severe consequences for tourism in the region, which relies on its spectacular calving. More widely, climate change has the potential to disrupt entirely the context within which economic and political decision making operates. Few people outside of science recognise the extreme rapidity with which climate can change, and the non-linear and dynamic nature of the climate system. Politicians have consistently failed to listen to the warnings or take them seriously. This means that climate change is likely to have some very unpleasant future surprises in store for us.

Looking at China

John Gittings

John Gittings looks beyond the rival images of 'economic miracle' and 'imminent collapse', and considers the deeper changes underway in China.

The question of where China may be heading looms ever larger today, as the country begins to be seen as a potential competitor in the unfolding twenty-first century to the world's only remaining superpower. It is by no means a new question: because of China's size and distance, because of the difficulty of understanding its distinctive culture, and because it often appears to offer an alternative mode of life (once Confucian, later Maoist, now a brand of market economy which does not yet have a name), the question 'Whither China?' has been a compelling one for several centuries. There is no record that Napoleon actually made the prediction attributed to him that 'when China wakes she will shake the world'. Nor did Zhou Enlai really ever observe, in a reverse aphorism, that it is 'too early to tell whether the French Revolution has succeeded'. (Neither for that matter does a Chinese curse exist that 'may you live in interesting times'.) This accretion of apocryphal sayings reflects the fascination and confusion surrounding China: 'The China Puzzle' is - too often - the default headline for lazy sub-editors putting a feature about the country on their page.

Today as in the past, views on China's future are wildly divergent. At one end of the spectrum there is the naive optimism expressed by Microsoft chairman Bill Gates who, speaking at the 2005 World Economic Forum, described the Chinese system as 'a brand-new form of capitalism … as a consumer it's the best thing that ever happened'. China's domination of the world market also impresses more sober observers, such as the *Financial Times*, which gave a recent supplement on China this headline: 'World is dancing to a Chinese tune: China's weight in global trade is so great that even a hiccup could shake some markets' (7.12.04).

At the other end of the spectrum is the dire prediction - as expressed in the title of a much-quoted book by critic Gordon Chang, *The Coming Collapse of China* - that this brand-new system risks catastrophic implosion. Its headlong economic growth is seen as fundamentally unstable, and as the source of dangerous new social tensions, while the failure of the Communist Party to match economic with political reform, it is argued, must condemn it to the fate, sooner rather than later, of the former Soviet and East European ruling parties.

This tendency on the part of the outside world to over-dramatise China goes back many decades, and in this article I intend to draw from my own experience of reporting over several decades, to discuss the obstacles to a clear understanding of China's recent past and future - and how these are seen by the Chinese themselves. Western opinion in the 1960s was largely polarised between those who regarded the Maoist approach as a wholly admirable 'brand-new system of socialism', and the cold-war view that China was, in effect, the world's first evil empire. Attitudes towards post-Mao China have been polarised in different ways: the US in particular has found it hard to decide whether a resurgent China is a shining example for the triumph of the market over ideology, or a looming threat to Western domination of that market, and whether in geo-strategic terms China should be regarded as a partner or competitor

Looking at Mao's China

The notion that one might write about mainland China without having visited the mainland was not considered unusual in the 1950s and 1960s. Only a small number of European students, mostly from the Scandinavian countries, had the opportunity to study in China: those from the US were limited to Taiwan or Hong Kong. Most of the material available for research into contemporary China existed in written form and often in English translation. The study of contemporary China could be treated in a way not dissimilar to the study of classical China. There was a limited corpus of available material and textual analysis was carried to a fine art.

China scholarship was set in the highly politicised context of a cold - sometimes hot - war in which the Beijing government was assigned, as time went on, an especially demonic role. A skein of links between government and the rapidly expanding field of 'area studies' did much to set the agenda for Western scholarship and journalism. The extent of this operation in the US came under attack during the Vietnam War from dissenting scholars, the Concerned Asian Scholars, who organised around the bulletin of that name. The subject was usefully revisited in a 1996 conference, the proceedings of which can be found on the web ('Asia, Asian Studies and the National Security State', *Bulletin of Concerned Asian Scholars*, vol.29, no.1, edited by Mark Selden).

This created a polarised approach in which it was hard to avoid being (or at least being categorised as) either 'for' or ' against' the new China. When I finally visited China for the first time in 1971, I travelled in a group from the UK-based Society for Anglo-Chinese Understanding (SACU), as a 'friend of China' not as a journalist, although I had already spent a decade writing on Chinese affairs. After five years of Cultural Revolution, visas for visiting Western journalists were unobtainable. Nevertheless the appetite then for even the most slender glimpse of China was enormous: I returned wearing a Mao cap and wrote a series of five articles for *The Guardian* which were run in full. We were able on such visits to record an element of idealism in the Cultural Revolution - which is generally brushed aside (not least by the Chinese themselves) today. Yet in retrospect we were too committed to allow ourselves to perceive the corrosive violence and the warping uniformity of Mao's cult. My own conclusion was fairly typical of that reached by many Western intellectuals at the time who sought to distance themselves from the prevailing cold war hostility towards China. The Thought of Mao Zedong was: 'not so much a cult of personality but more a collective way of life, which provides the moral imperatives for the youth of China who will inherit Mao's revolution' (*The Guardian*, 30 April 1971).

Looking at Deng's China

In 1972 Kissinger and Nixon re-opened the door to Beijing, and the 'Chinese menace' soon waned. Access now became less difficult for Western scholars, journalists and, before long, for language students. The death of Mao in 1976 and the subsequent repudiation of the Cultural Revolution, coupled with the establishment of full diplomatic relations with the US in 1979, made it possible for the Deng Xiaoping regime to be labelled as 'pragmatic'. Foreign observers looked for continuity, and foreign diplomats had a vested interest in predicting it. For them, the most important changes were taking place in external policy, where China had formed an opportunistic entente with the West against the Soviet Union, and in the new opportunities for foreign business offered by the Special Economic Zones and Joint Ventures. Unlike the samizdat-writing dissidents in the Soviet Union, China's Democracy Wall activists (1979-80) won no vocal support from Western political leaders.

Yet the 1980s was the golden time for reporting from China and there was a real desire to know along which road the Chinese would now move. It was not yet taken for granted that China had entirely forsaken Mao's road to socialism: many Chinese officials stressed that moral incentives would continue as well as those of the new material kind. In spite of the abolition of the people's communes, rural leaders also talked of the need to maintain a balance between public and private interest.

The political scene grew increasingly lively as reform-minded scholars, with some encouragement from the Party Secretary-general Hu Yaobang, discussed the cult of personality, the alienation of the masses from the Party, and the need for internal Party democracy. Others, both in the leadership and at the grassroots, opposed arguments which seemed to undermine Mao's socialist vision and to diminish their own prerogatives. The tensions which these arguments generated led to the dismissal of Hu in 1987, and to the student protests on his death two years later which raised even more fundamental questions and resulted in the crackdown of Tiananmen Square. Regrettably, the intellectual ferment of the 1980s was often under-rated by Western commentators, who failed to fully appreciate an argument still conducted largely in Marxist terms. And even as the army moved in to Beijing, foreign diplomats could be heard to argue that the students 'don't know what they mean by democracy'.

The Beijing Massacre changed the terms of reference under which China was reported in the West and - to a lesser extent - the way in which the ruling regime was viewed by Western governments. After the relative optimism of the 1980s, the reactionary backlash of the old guard in the leadership was a dismal shock. What happened on the night of 3-4 June 1989 (and on subsequent days when random killings continued), and the repression of the next several years, seemed to present a definitively negative answer to all those questions about whether the Communist Party could accommodate itself to peaceful political change. Western governments who had previously shrugged off complaints about human rights abuses were now compelled to take them seriously, at least for public consumption. (In private, some of their officials shared the impatience of one Beijing-based British diplomat with the human rights pressure groups and their 'little lists of names' (of imprisoned dissidents)).

Yet the changes set in motion, deliberately or otherwise, by the reforms of the 1980s continued to gather pace: there was more social mobility and more entrepreneurial activity, as well as more crime and corruption. Those former students who put economic development in first place joined the flow heading for the economic zones on the coast. After Deng Xiaoping had embarked on his Southern Expedition and kick-started the economic revolution back to life in 1993 - and in a higher gear too - the tentative political reforms of the 1980s began to appear dated and, as a new urban boom developed, irrelevant. Mr Deng's foray confirmed beyond doubt that China was taking the capitalist road: no one talked any longer of a return to 'genuine' socialist alternatives, and there was no longer any question about the destination. The speed of Chinese economic progress swept all before it: as British prime minister John Major remarked, when told that it was generating significant social problems, 'there can't be much wrong with eight per cent GDP growth'.

At the same time, the collapse of the Soviet-led bloc left China without a clear strategic value to the West. In the positive view, China was a living workshop for the attractiveness of the globalised market-economy model now being pressed upon the rest of the world by those countries which already dominated it. On the other hand, China's economic success might translate itself in the future into political and military strength which could pose a threat to those same interests. A new set of images began to appear on the front covers of Western news magazines, embodying a mixture of admiration and fear at the Chinese advance. To quote the headline to a *New York Times Magazine* special feature in 1996: 'The 21st Century Starts Here: China Booms. The World Holds Its Breath'.

Looking at China since Deng

Attitudes towards the emerging Chinese superpower (I prefer to call it half a superpower) have become increasingly schizophrenic since the late 1990s. In a global media dominated by the US, this reflects to a large extent new complications in US-China relations, as well as mixed feelings about China's economic growth. But it also responds to real contradictory pulls and pushes in Chinese society as it becomes more diverse and yet remains confined by a political culture which is increasingly out-of-date. The task facing us is thus twofold: to recognise and discount the hidden biases of Western perceptions, and to identify real changes and perceptions within China, where, in spite of sporadic censorship, there is now a lively debate about the future.

A view of 'Chinese communism' with its origins in the cold war era still persists in the analyses of some right-wing and/or pro-Taiwan scholars and analysts, and often spills over into mainstream journalism. This became particularly noticeable in coverage of US-China relations in the late 1990s and early 2000s, when things were complicated by the transition from the Clinton to the Bush administration. During Bill Clinton's visit to China in June 1998 the media at first had focused upon the plight of Chinese political dissidents, but they subsequently took a generally complacent view after the president was allowed to call for democracy in an address broadcast live on national Chinese television. The White House's simplistic view that Mr Clinton had established a special rapport with President Jiang Zemin was widely echoed: in fact, Mr Jiang clamped down within months upon the fledgling Chinese Democracy Party.

A year later, in the aftermath of the US bombing of the Chinese embassy in Belgrade during the Kosovo war, there was little sympathy for China, which was frequently accused of over-reacting. The stage-managed character of Chinese anti-US demonstrations received more attention than the genuine anger which they reflected - and which the Chinese government's control measures sought partly to contain. Western coverage tended to miss the real point - that in spite of this provocation the Jiang regime was determined to maintain, if at all possible, good relations with the US. (While there were 'ups and downs' in US-China relations, said the *People's Daily*, friendly ties between them were 'of great importance to the whole world'.)

Chinese reaction to the incident in April 2001 when a US spy plane made a forced landing on Hainan island was again looked at through a critical American lens. Coverage missed the point that Beijing remained committed to improving US-China relations, and that a wide range of popular views (including some that criticised the government for being too soft) was being expressed. Chinese reaction to the 11 September 2001 terrorist attack on New York was also subjected to misinterpretation. By its usual standards, the Chinese media reported the attack with unusual speed, and official condolences were quickly sent. Popular opinion on the street, and on the Chinese internet chatrooms, was more varied, with some expressing the view that the US had only got what it deserved. Yet Western commentators were too quick to reproach Beijing for an alleged lack of sympathy: the *Wall Street Journal* even accused 'an isolated China (of) seek(ing) friends among the rogue nations of the world'.

In reality Beijing wanted to maintain the momentum of improved US-China relations after the spy plane crisis, and had its own domestic reasons to support an international 'war against terror'. Chinese leaders were quietly satisfied that the Bush administration now had a 'real enemy' on which to focus, instead of demonising China, as several prominent neo-conservative figures in Washington had done since the inauguration. Thus 11 September was described by the *People's Daily* as 'a turning-point in the post-cold war pattern', and Beijing took advantage of it to step up repression, with tacit US approval, of its own (mostly peaceful) Muslim separatists in North-west China.

Looking at China's future

So, Whither China, amid all the contradictions and misperceptions that have so complicated the task of analysis in the past, and still do today? We must of course start with the Communist Party, although with a different perspective from that of the neo-cold warriors. Contrary to the general view, the Party is now stronger than it was in the 1980s, even though it is also more unpopular; but it is no longer even vestigially 'communist'. While many people in China will casually (and openly) denounce the Party as corrupt and undemocratic, this often means little more than similar complaints in democratic countries that no politician can be trusted.

The Communist Party

The Party has achieved its current position by the following means:

♦ It has completed the *rejection* of a socialist project, while most of those who advocated such a project have retired or died. Its aim now is straightforwardly to deliver the material goods to the Chinese people by whatever means work best: this is the well-understood meaning of such official formulae as the doctrine of the 'Three Represents' propounded by Deng's successor Jiang Zemin.

♦ It has *redefined* itself as a 'ruling' rather than a 'communist' party. This shift is not just a question of semantics but reflects sustained discussion among Party theorists on how to re-legitimise the Party's leading role. A ruling party (perhaps the term is better rendered as 'governing') holds power not because it represents particular classes or embodies a particular project but because it can satisfy the here-and-now requirements of society as a whole. In this respect the concept has something in common with the old notion of a 'mandate' which could be withdrawn if the emperor failed to deliver.

♦ There has been a large-scale *re-composition* of the Party's membership. While it remains a substantial force numerically (around five per cent of total population - a much higher percentage therefore of all adults), it is now more representative of the urban business interests and professional intelligentsia who control or run the Chinese economy. This process was formalised when the 16th Party Congress in 2002 amended the constitution to allow private entrepreneurs to join the Party (many already had).

Social unrest

Social unrest presents another paradox: there is vastly more protest and dissatisfaction than in the 1980s, among a sizeable sector of marginalised population: the main categories are the peasants living in depressed rural areas, away from the coast or other booming provincial centres, and the 'laid-off workers' from state industries which have gone bankrupt or have been semi-privatised and asset-stripped. This unrest features prominently amongst proponents of regime collapse scenarios: a figure of 58,000 protests across the country in 2003, involving some three million people, is quoted. Yet this poses less of a threat than would have been the case if similarly largely sectors of population had been disaffected in the past, for a number of reasons:

♦ The forces of repression in the rural areas - police, militia and enlisted hoodlums - are effective, particularly in more remote and deprived locations where those running the state apparatus have a vested interest in defending their privileges. This also strengthens the belief (often an illusion) among peasant protesters that, as in the old days, their troubles stem from local oppression, and that the Party/Emperor in Beijing is not to blame.

♦ Labour protest tends to be based on single work units, or at best in single urban locations, and is rarely organised on a wider basis. This is partly because the state makes it clear that it will not tolerate any protest engaging in *chuanlian* (the phrase used by Red Guards in the Cultural Revolution when they 'made contacts' across the country). It also reflects the self-contained nature of work communities and the posing of demands based on self-interest rather than a broader solidarity.

♦ Many protests which observe the rules (i.e. do not exceed local boundaries) do get results of a sort - although this happens more often in urban than rural environments. A regime that has made 'social stability' its top priority is more willing to buy off protestors: back wages and pensions may be paid (though rarely in full); a few corrupt officials may be punished; emergency funds may be allocated; and some attempt made to deal with housing and welfare problems. In the disadvantaged rural areas, there has been some success in lessening the burden of illegal tax impositions, and the focus of complaint is now shifting towards the misappropriation of land by speculators with good 'connections' in local government.

Social change

China is, to put it very crudely, a large enough country for considerable zones of poverty and protest to exist without their impinging too visibly or effectively upon the more dynamic areas of economic enrichment and social change. This might appear to be a scenario for an updated version of Mao's revolutionary strategy in which the 'towns' of capitalist development will be encircled and overwhelmed by the 'countryside' of the marginalised and poor. However the 'towns' are no longer islands of prosperity, but have spread out, ink-blot fashion, to cover very sizeable areas of the adjacent 'countryside'. (Rural suburbs of many major cities now enjoy a quasi-urban lifestyle.) And over the past two decades, better communications, education and the loosening of population controls have led to much greater social mobility. The so-called 'independent kingdoms' of the past - isolated areas where resistance could fester unobserved - no longer exist on the scale required to become reservoirs of revolution.

Migrant labour is a critical factor in the social transformation of this 'countryside': at a rough estimate, between 100 and 130 million adults who are still registered in the rural areas - up to ten per cent of the entire Chinese population - are currently working away from home for months or years at a time. (Many will only return to their families once a year at the Chinese New Year Festival - assuming that their employers have paid them the wages they are owed.) This is clearly a potential source of instability if such a vast labour force were one day to find no work, but at present it is more of a stabilising factor, and not just because of the cash remittances from migrants to their families. Although urban in-migration is tightly controlled, some long-term migrants do become urbanised: the majority who eventually return home take with them new entrepreneurial skills and ideas, which help to diversify rural life.

While some (though by no means all) rural areas remain as 'backward' as before, if not more so, the urban and semi-urban landscape is very different. A social transformation since the mid-1990s has made tens of millions increasingly autonomous from the Party, with their own aspirations and demands. The most visible signs of this shift have been at the material level, as a new middle class expresses its priorities for consumption and acquisition, unfettered by any fear of political disapproval. Of equal importance, millions now in their everyday lives articulate goals and values across a whole range of issues - from sexual relationships to citizens' rights - with a high degree of freedom. As is often explained to visiting foreigners, especially those with experience of previous decades, 'we can say what we like now - though we can't always put it in print'. On the negative side, the loosening of Party authority, together with the spread of corruption, has encouraged new destructive forces in society, of which the saddest example has been the rapid spread of prostitution, human trafficking, and drug abuse.

The environment

This is China's hidden time-bomb. The Dengist strategy, continued by his successors, of maintaining a high rate of economic growth while encouraging the market to run rip, has secured popular acquiescence in continued Party rule at a very high price in terms of environmental exploitation. The surge in Chinese output and consumption in the 1990s redoubled the pressure on natural resources that, in many areas, had already been undermined by unwise policies in the Maoist era. The basic essentials which support human life -

reliable water, sufficient tree cover, and fertile earth - have all come under increasing strain. The devastating floods of 1998 were caused by a combination of deforestation in tributary areas upstream, and conversion of traditional floodlands for new building and agriculture in the middle valley. They were followed by the drought of 2000. These disasters were two sides of the same ecological problem - both caused by the excessive exploitation of water resources.

In such projects as the high-profile Three Gorges Dam on the Yangtze river, and in other equally large but less well-known hydraulic enterprises, the government remains committed to the 'big dam philosophy'; and in this it has the support of the World Bank, which (while careful not to endorse the controversial Three Gorges project) financed an earlier dam at Xiaolangdi on the Yellow River. Work has now begun on an even more stupendous engineering enterprise - to transfer water from the Yangtze to the Yellow River by three separate routes: no debate has been allowed on this project, and its effect on the environment is unpredictable.

Reform and repression

It has been a truism now for a decade and a half that political reform has lagged a long way behind economic reform. Even the fairly modest proposals for inner-Party democracy and public supervision of government made during the 1980s have been ignored. The one innovation has been village elections, but these are limited to the lowest level. In Marxist-Maoist terms (which the Chinese Party no longer employs), reform of the political superstructure has lagged an exceedingly long way behind the transformation of the economic base. Hopes are raised before successive Party congresses that a new regime will begin to redress the balance, and soon are dashed again: the time, it is always claimed, is not yet ripe. In 2004-5 it is the turn of Party leader Hu Jintao and state Premier Wen Jiabao, who had been seen as more responsive to popular aspirations than Jiang Zemin (Deng Xiaoping's successor), to disappoint expectations. Their nervous handling in January 2005 of the death of former Party secretary-general Zhao Ziyang (Jiang's predecessor, who had been under virtual house arrest since opposing the 1989 crack-down) confirmed that the long-anticipated 'Beijing thaw' was still an illusion.

The periodic purging of outspoken newspapers such as the popular

Southern Weekend, the censorship of sensitive stories, the imprisonment of lone dissident voices, and the harassment of the brave mothers of Tiananmen Square who still seek justice for their fallen sons and daughters, are symptomatic of a regime which - while berating Japan for failing to acknowledge the past record of aggression in China - still refuses to come to terms with its own past. The persecution of the Falun Gong, which unwisely provoked the wrath of Jiang Zemin by demonstrating outside his front door in 1999, is also brutal and unnecessary. (The Falun Gong is a cultish organisation led from abroad by a 'Master', who expounds a questionable doctrine, but it is no threat to the Chinese state.)

Yet these examples of high-profile repression are only one aspect of a complex political culture which at a less formal level has become much more variegated. There is far more argument and debate in China today, much of it challenging to Party orthodoxies, than the headlines over Western news stories reporting the latest 'crack-down on dissent' would suggest. The internet has played a significant role here, allowing the circulation of information and ideas in a less visible form, one which does not so readily provoke censorship. Even the *People's Daily* website is more outspoken than the print version of the Party's official newspaper. In spite of controls and censorship, the internet allows the circulation of information and discussion of sensitive issues among millions of younger Chinese, as well as within the academic world. Such issues include the widening gap between rich and poor, official corruption, discrimination against migrant workers, and HIV-AIDS. Some material is even copied from overseas websites run by dissident Chinese, to which direct access is banned.

As the state comes to rely more upon professional managers and technocrats to run its vast enterprise, and less upon the 'intellectuals' once employed to provide and bolster ideologically correct theory, the latter have become more autonomous and more like their counterparts in the West (with whom they have much closer relationships). The recent publication by Verso of *One China, Many Paths* (2004) gives us, for the first time in English, a fascinating glimpse into the diversity of their arguments. Editor Wang Chaohua writes of 'an international field of communication and exchange ... that now extends from the mainland to Hong Kong, Taiwan and Singapore, the US and Australia, with outposts in Japan and Europe'.

The debate is no longer, as it was in the 1980s, between unreconstructed

Maoism and semi-socialist reform: it is between unfettered marketisation, whose partisans often endorse exploitation and corruption as necessary for progress, and the advocacy of some sort of social agenda which might humanise China's new order in the global economy. China's entry into the WTO in 2002 marked the apogee of the marketeers' forward march: for a while the air rang with claims that China now enjoyed a 'level playing field' on the global market, and that everyone would benefit from a 'win plus win' outcome. But there is a growing realisation that China's WTO entry was bound to accelerate social polarisation, with the richer provinces and the economic elite with superior business knowledge being better able to maximise their advantages. Questions about the future of the Communist Party are part of the debate, although they are put more circumspectly. It is easier to assert that the Party 'cannot last for another 100 years' than to put a finer time limit on its existence. Rather than explicit arguments for a multi-party system, there are calls for the introduction of electoral politics within the Party itself, with the implication that it will remain the dominant political force, but only after gaining popular consent.

So what are the prospects of the 'collapse of China'? The phrase is not as imprecise as it may sound, for the sudden implosion of the Party could, in the view of most Chinese, including many political exiles, be a disaster for the whole country. Wang Dan, a leading activist from Tiananmen Square, hopes there is a good chance instead of the Party's 'evolution into something different'. And Wang Chaohua, also a former activist, believes that the present regime could adapt itself to last 'for another twenty years'. Of course there are too many unknown variables ahead - not all of them within China's control - for us to be able to rule out a more catastrophic scenario. One variable is the speed of environmental degradation, which could increase rapidly through mistaken policies, or the effect of global warming, or both. Another unknown is the future of the global market, which currently underpins such a significant element of Chinese employment. A third possibility, not as far-fetched as it may seem, would be conflict in the Taiwan Straits involving the US, as a result of miscalculation by the Chinese or Taiwan governments, or both. However, looking at China from outside, we would do well to avoid the stark dichotomy between 'collapse' and 'miracle', and focus instead on the deeper changes underway in Chinese society, which are likely to transform the landscape over time less dramatically, but just as radically.

Sailing towards the icebergs

New Labour's third term

Michael Rustin

Michael Rustin *argues that many difficult issues lie in wait for the new Labour government, and threaten to fragment its fragile base of support. What is needed is a renewed model of a democratic state, working on both national and international planes, which can address, negotiate and manage the destructive consequences of global market forces, according to values of democratic citizenship.*

Waking up

It took only a few days after the General Election - with its satisfactory outcome of a smaller Labour majority, and the progress of parties to the left of Labour - for one's initial feeling of hopefulness to be dispelled. In the aftermath of this narrow victory, we needed a period of reflection and negotiation between the different tendencies, within and outside the party, that have sustained the government thus far. The problem is how to refashion and develop the broad compromise which has sustained the New Labour government for the last eight years (before its derailment by Iraq), between the commitment on the one hand to a competitive capitalist economy, and on the other to an extension of social justice, and of a sphere of universal public provision. In the campaign, Labour asked the electorate to forget about the Iraq crisis, and to reward its domestic success in bringing unbroken economic growth, near full-employment, and a significant expansion of expenditure on certain public services (together with its proposals, of dubious electoral appeal, to 'modernise' these on market-oriented lines). This compromise has throughout been the basis of the power-sharing agreement between Blair and Brown. It was fortunate therefore that Blair was obliged early in the election campaign, by necessity rather than choice, to reaffirm his partnership with Brown, whose continued central role in the government, and probably eventual succession as its leader, was thus declared. For three weeks Blair and Brown appeared inseparable.

If what we needed after the election was reflection, what we actually got was a return to business-as-usual, with nothing learned and nothing forgotten. From the Parliamentary left there was an immediate challenge to Blair's leadership, impossible to contemplate at that moment. The Blairites announced in Thatcherite terms that there would be 'no turning back', and immediately set about mimicking Howard's electoral populism with the idea of Guantanamo-style uniforms for offenders doing community services, and prohibitions of certain teenage headwear. The Queen's Speech pressed on with the New Labour commitment to privatisation in the supply of health and education services, and proposed many measures to instil more social order and discipline (misnamed respect). Identity cards were to the fore. The regulation of the the poor has always been a New Labour theme, but it is perverse to read the election outcome as a demand for this. The Tory law and order campaign, after all, had failed, and was being abandoned even as New Labour took it up again. The programme for the new Parliament also made much of reducing the numbers on incapacity benefit (about two million), in effect proposing to extend the scope of earlier 'welfare to work' programmes, which attach entitlements to benefits more forcefully to the obligation to work. But though problems of work availability were given little attention (many of those receiving incapacity benefit are casualties of the decline of mining and manufacturing), the initial tone of those proposals was cautious.

Looking backwards: the May election campaign

The election campaign should have prepared one for this generally dire start. A Labour Party which cannot use a general election as an opportunity to prepare electors for the longer term, and as an occasion for reflection and public education, is unlikely to re-invent these talents in the shock of losing much of its majority. None of the three parties was able to put forward a convincing view of how Britain should be governed for the next five years. This is why none of them came out of the election successfully. The argument of an earlier article (*Soundings* 28, p118) was borne out, that we are in one of Gramsci's famous periods in which the old is dead, and the new is struggling to be born, a situation in which a variety of 'morbid symptoms' appears.

In fact, the success up to the election of New Labour's version of the mixed economy - market-led but with improved public services - was such that neither the Conservatives nor the Liberal Democrats dared to diverge. Labour was standing not on what it intended to do, but what it had already done. 'Don't let the Tories ruin it' was its theme.

On the margins of this provisional settlement, safe for the moment while growth continued and health and education received their cash injection, the Tories campaigned on anxiety and resentment, expressing resentment at their exile from power, and the anxieties of those in the electorate who feel excluded from the benefits of modernisation and prosperity. Never was a campaign so exclusively focused on discipline and repression - asylum seekers, refugees, criminals, gypsies, the MRSA superbug and dirt itself figured as the enemies to be brought under control, and the return of Matron was the mildest solution offered. The Tories seemed to be targeting the downwardly mobile, against both the Lib Dems' and Labour's appeal to the upwardly mobile. No wonder, at a time of prosperity, that they lost to the two combined by 60-40.

The Liberal Democrats chipped away at the consensus from the other side. High-minded, and identifying with the moderately comfortable as strongly as the Tories courted the fearful, the Lib Dems offered their 'responsible opposition' to the Iraq war, a decent position on civil liberties, and a commitment to a fairer tax-system - which was, however, less radical than it appeared to be. It is desirable to tax incomes over £100,000 at 50 per cent, and valuable to have put that commitment on the agenda, but the proceeds of the tax were to be deployed not in the broader cause of social justice, but to cherry-pick two specific constituencies - the student vote, through the commitment to abolish tuition fees, and those pensioners with savings who would benefit from free social care.

The superficial closeness to one another of the three parties, focusing as they all did on specific pledges of this or that kind, and offering little by way of broader programme, was misleading, in the same way that the apparent convergence between American Democrats and Republicans has been. The parties remain different in their main constituencies of support, and in their informing ideologies, even though New Labour's focus on 'Middle Britain' might

'none of the three parties was able to put forward a convincing view of how Britain should be governed for the next five years'

suggest otherwise. Whereas parties used to confront each other with markedly different programmes, but then converged once subject to the pressures of office (remember Wilson and Heath), the opposite now obtains. When the environment is stable and the electorate broadly contented, parties offer minimal changes, but

nevertheless harbour the intention of remaking the world in their own image if they can entrench themselves in power for long enough. This was the Tory project (with its 'lower tax' advocates kept tactically out of sight, but not out of mind, in the campaign). Given the advance of Labour's second term programme over its first (in its public spending plans at least), one hoped that this was true of some of them too. The alternation of parties has become a longer game, and that is why it is important now to be thinking already about the election of 2009 or 2010. But the early omens are far from promising. After all, prior to the election Blair seemed set on pushing Brown out, not on his planned succession to 10 Downing Street. Conversion to the ways of party consensus may have come to Blair on the road to Westminster, but then again it may not. The divisions over Iraq have damaged the party's capacity to think long-term about the future. So we return to the old ground, more mindless modernisation by the Blairites, and clarity about what they *don't* want from the Labour left, but little new thinking about what they *do*. Gordon Brown's position is as yet not fully discernible (though his scheme to help those with low incomes get a foot on the housing ladder was different from the law and order emphasis which dominated elsewhere).

The fact of Labour's achieving a third victory - indeed an unimaginable prospect ten years ago - reminds one of how successful it was, until Iraq, in constructing its inclusive 'big tent', its version of hegemony achieved from the centre. It has for the time being become almost the party of big business, or at least a government of which the business class has no present fear. Thus Digby Anderson, Director-General of the CBI, intervened in mid-campaign to declare that large firms would not tolerate the Conservatives' capping of immigration, a blow to Howard from an unlikely source. The *FT* offered its now-customary cautious support to Labour, and its columnist Martin Wolf said he would like to see Gordon Brown's model compromise between market-led growth and social inclusion tested out for a further four years. Rupert Murdoch repaid, through the *Sun*'s endorsement of New Labour, Tony Blair's many accommodations with him, which have included Labour's pro-Sky media policies, its philo-American Iraq adventure, and its nil progress on integration within Europe. And on the other side of the labour-capital divide, the trade unions were fully supportive, especially as Labour agreed to put aside its plans for later retirement until after the election. Until Iraq, very few social constituencies had become seriously hostile to the government; disturbances such as the petrol tanker drivers' strike in 2000, the mishandled foot and mouth disease epidemic of 2001, the crisis of the railways following the spate of serious accidents, and last year's battle over fox-hunting were all shrugged off without too much damage to Labour's poll ratings.

But the campaign showed the New Labour project starting to unravel. It seemed remarkably difficult for Labour to raise public interest in its plans for the next term, even though one of them, universal child care provision, should be a major advance for the welfare system. But it is impossible for a left-of-centre party in Britain to govern for long if it alienates its main liberal constituency, as New Labour has done in its foreign policy, and in its approach to civil liberties. Stuart Hall ('New Labour's Double-Shuffle', *Soundings* 24) has described the key role of 'spin' in managing the domestic contradictions of New Labour's pro-capitalist programme. In the election we saw its catastrophic failure to manage the tensions in its Iraq policy, as these masters of the media found their agenda taken over by leaked advice from the Attorney General which would have been better placed in the public domain months or years before. (As usual, the failed cover-up does more damage than the original crime.)

Although the relative success of Labour in the Midlands and North showed that Gordon Brown's cautious redistribution of income had achieved some recognition among working people, the low polls and lukewarm support achieved even in these 'core' areas means alarm for the future, should the economy turn-down and the Tories recover their effectiveness. The fact that a reasonable overall majority of 66 seats was achieved with only a 36 per cent share of the vote (6 points down from 2001) is a further source of concern. The majority is apparently good enough for the next Parliament, but it is a poor base from which to seek a further victory in 2009 and 2010.

The Blair-Brown question

I must confess to having felt an unexpected sympathy for Tony Blair as the campaign progressed to its conclusion, and as the results were announced through the night. *Soundings* has been arguing against Blairite 'modernisation' for the whole of its existence, and we were opposed to Blair's Iraq War alliance with the neoconservative administration in Washington. However, watching the battering he was receiving during the election, and his resilience in face of it, I was put more in mind for once of his achievements and virtues than of his failures and vices. New Labour's success has created some space for a more progressive politics, as the 'second term' agenda of higher public spending has shown. And Blair's appeal to non-Labour constituencies, and his effectiveness until the Iraq crisis in managing the modes of modern media and celebrity politics, has contributed greatly to Labour's electoral success. The evidence may indicate that with Gordon Brown as its Prime Ministerial candidate Labour would have achieved a larger majority than it did, but appearances may not be all that they seem. In any case, a larger Labour majority, under whomsoever, was by no means what was needed at this point.

Attacks on leaders of centre-left parties are liable to be over-determined. Their proponents make whatever use they can of a leader's weaknesses and failures, and seek to detach support as much from within a leader's own party as from that of his opponents, whose hostility can be taken for granted. Observing Howard's character assassination of Blair, one recalled the Republicans' eight-year campaign to destroy Clinton, and its ultimate triumph, since Clinton's consequent unavailability to the Democrats' presidential campaign is one of the factors that cost the Democrats the 2000 and 2004 elections. We can see what an extraordinary electoral asset Clinton was to the Democrats from the feebleness of his successors. We can be certain that the day Gordon Brown succeeds Blair, if he does, all efforts will be made to demonstrate that he is a lumbering figure with feet of clay. To escape his labelling as an old Scottish socialist, he will be pushed to show that he is no less conservative than Blair. Most of those who attacked Blair in the election did so because they believed and hoped that Brown would not succeed. Even without a change of leadership, the left stands to gain from the shift in power which appeared to follow from Blair's renewed dependence on Brown, and his announced retirement some time in the next term. It would be best to reflect carefully on this development, with the prospects for the next election of 2009 as the main consideration. One certainly needs to see a different equilibrium of power in the Labour Party. But this was never likely to be achieved by the expedient of summarily knocking over one of the two pillars on which it has depended throughout.

Sailing towards the icebergs: prospects for the third term

What prospect or programme does the Labour Party, or the broader left, have to offer for the five or so years to come? Indeed, does it have one? What was on offer in the campaign, a *status quo* of continued economic prosperity and 'modernised' public services, was more a retrospective description of Labour's second term than a vision for its third. It is possible now to see New Labour as a complacent political Titanic sailing off towards the icebergs. Striking about Labour's campaign was its determined avoidance of difficult issues. As Shirley Williams said on one of Andrew Neil's late-night talk shows, the Labour Party hoped that the people would stay comfortably asleep during the election, and that passive satisfaction would get them through - as indeed it did, just about.

The problem in building or maintaining a consensus or hegemony is that issues as they arise - 'events, dear boy', as Macmillan put it - bring contradictions and divisions. With a majority of 66, and two rival parties in better shape than before, these can no longer be bridged by 'spin' as they were before, especially as trust and confidence has been so eroded by the misuse of these. (The deceptions accompanying the decision to go to war were as much the cause of voters' defection from Labour as the war itself. This is why the Attorney General's advice of two years earlier still mattered.) The key issues, and their implications for the sustaining of a progressive democratic consensus, need now to be identified. This is the longer-term analytic and programmatic work that *Soundings* was in part founded to do.

My view is that the government needs both to sustain the broad compromise on which it was first elected, *and* respond more forcefully to the needs of its broader left-of-centre constituencies, as it did in its second term compared with its first. Compromises and settlements are a moving frontier - sometimes very rapidly moving as under Thatcher. Especially when the broad coalition has suffered serious damage (Iraq) it is urgent to grasp how it can now be repaired and strengthened. What is to be the equivalent in its third term of the second term's expansion and improvement of health and education services, and its full-employment and anti-poverty programmes? More of the same will not do. No sign of such a new vision was to be seen from start to finish of Labour's election campaign.

What are the problems that the government is going to face, which it has been so reluctant to talk about? They include the problems of climate change and the environment, the implications of longer life-spans for pension provision, the growing crisis of transport, and increasing regional inequalities in Britain. There are also the unresolved issues of Britain's relationship with the United States and with Europe, and the damage the Blair government has done to the conception of a negotiated and lawful international order through its support for United States' unilateralism in Iraq.

All of these issues are potentially divisive, threatening to further fragment Labour's support. The benefits of an effective policy to reduce carbon emissions will be experienced in the future, while its costs will be felt at once. It is not an enviable task for a government committed to prosperity and improved opportunities to have, for instance, to curtail the growth of air travel by taxing aviation fuel. Cheap air travel is a huge boon to many, yet it is also one of the major contributors to global warming. Road congestion and the increased use of the motor car raise similar issues. Enhanced recycling also brings short-term costs in time and effort, and requires the exercise of responsibility. Choices between new nuclear power stations, conspicuous wind-farms, and higher fuel taxes to encourage conservation are also hard ones, arousing antagonisms. Similarly, government is going to have to enhance savings for old age, and extend working lives, since people live longer after their retirement now than in the past, so that wage earners will have to save more to avoid their impoverishment in old age. The development of education and child-care services now involves major choices about the balance between parental and paid working roles, and between person-centred and market-centred conceptions of childhood, which remain unconsidered.

Moving on

It is not that there is any simple or ideological solution to any of these issues. The fact is, however, that all of them challenge the idea that economic growth led by the market and consumer choice can simply continue into the indefinite future, with no significant changes or adjustments. Thus ideas about 'wealth' and 'well-being' need to be re-addressed and rethought, since it is unlikely that present economic growth rates can be indefinitely sustained, and evident that growth itself does not equate in any simple way with satisfied and satisfying lives. It is because it cannot be that everything will continue as it has that the country seems to have sleepwalked through the recent election, as the parties colluded in turning a blind eye to these painful realities.

What is required to address such issues is a government and party (and many others) committed to clarifying them, and to seeking consensus about their solutions. Government must not be afraid to use its democratically assigned powers when these are necessary to address 'market failures', just as it has sought to tackle the 'non-market failures' of 'old welfare state' provision. Whereas New Labour's fervour over the past few years has been about the benefits that markets can bring in fields from which they have been hitherto excluded, what it should now be thinking about is the unsustainable effects of and damage caused by market forces. It is not a return to 'traditional socialism' that is wanted, but its reinvention to deal with these new conditions of turbulence and uncertainty, and the distributive dilemmas, including increasing inequalities, which arise from them. The situation requires enhanced democratic responsibility, deliberative planning, and the attention to the just distribution of costs and benefits, things which have always been central to democratic socialist politics. How else are these looming icebergs to be avoided? These are the debates about policy and programme that the Labour government and its allies should have been having, linking these concrete problems of local and global market failure to its underlying principles and its theories of agency, including the key agency of a modernised state. These debates need to go well beyond government and the Labour Party, especially since the agencies and institutions which have done most to explore these issues - climate change and the environment, for example - have emerged from social movements remote from government.

There are general principles which need to underpin these debates. Democracy is the first. The government's new majority lacks democratic legitimacy, as everyone except its spokespersons can see, and this will deprive it of moral authority to deal with divisive issues when they arise, whatever the parliamentary whips may do. Labour should reform the system, making it more proportional, in order to increase both voter participation, and the perceived justice of election outcomes. The lower participation becomes, the greater is the bias of the political system to the right, as the American experience shows.[1] Labour should be worrying about winning the support of those who do not vote, as well as fishing in the pool of those who do. Its purpose should be to ensure the entrenchment of a new social settlement, not its own indefinite rule, and electoral reform has an essential role in this.

The second principle is equality. The management of unavoidable conflicts, and the bearing of inescapable costs and readjustments in the face of global realities, is not possible without a sense of shared citizenship and social membership, and this cannot be achieved in a society in which inequality is growing. Social responsibility depends on recognition and reciprocity, and cannot be achieved primarily by coercive means, as levels of violence and incarceration in the United States compared with European societies make clear. Social solidarity is undermined by the social segregation, envy and guilt which arises from inequalities which are perceived as unjust. Nor is 'equal opportunity' a feasible goal unless the gradient of inequality becomes less steep. The ideology of the United States gives more emphasis to opportunity than any other society, yet its rates of social mobility are lower than those of more equal societies. Conservative populism thrives, as we see, when democratic institutions seem weak, and when resentment of inequality and injustice is high.

These issues of democratic citizenship also have their implications for the micro-politics of civil society, and the macro-politics of the globe. The

---

1. Ben Rogers (*Guardian*, 14.5.05) advocated compulsory voting on similar grounds, that the voting electorate was increasingly now skewed towards the better off, and Geoff Harcourt made such a proposal in *Soundings* 16. This is a good idea, though probably harder to win even than PR.

continuing arguments about the meaning and purpose of the public sector in which *Soundings* has extensively engaged are one sphere in which the meaning of citizenship is daily determined. Modes of regulation (the 'audit culture'), the recognition or denial of complexity, a capacity to attend to dimensions of feeling, all affect people's experiences as producers or consumers of services, and influence their quality. New Labour has been at risk of imposing an ideology of consumer markets no less one-dimensional than state socialist bureaucracy was. It seems now to be committed to a new version of state capitalism, in which capital, which has not been too successful in holding its own in many global markets, is offered access to protected markets within the public sphere. Compromises are being effected here, both with private sector producers, and with a segment of consumers, via an agenda of 'choice' whose purpose is to hold the affluent within the public sector at the cost of greater stratification of provision within it. Crucial to the next few years is whether the debate about 'modernisation' can become more open and thoughtful than it has been hitherto, in regard to the optimal mix of state and market - and 'exit, voice and loyalty'[2] - in the organisation of and delivery of services.

It does not seem possible for a left-of-centre government to succeed in the long run on the basis on deep internal divisions about its international policy. (Recall the lasting damage that the Vietnam War did to the American Democrats.) The reason for the high levels of disillusionment over the Iraq War was that it went against the liberal belief that the international order needs to be managed through law and negotiation, not by the unilateral exercise of force. Here was another fundamental issue avoided during the election, the contradictions between alignment with neo-cons in Washington, and engagement with a democratic Europe; between the aims of climate change, debt relief, and constructive address to the problems of Africa and the Middle East, and the positions of the US Administration. The repressive 'anti-terrorism' agenda (which includes identity cards) is another product of the government's subservience to Washington's view of the world. Blair asks that people should 'move on' from Iraq. Indeed, but the question is the direction in which we should move. This is perhaps the largest of all the icebergs.

Although it is not always recognised, there was a coherent theoretical

---

2. These three terms are Albert Hirschman's, from *Exit, Voice and Loyalty* (1970).

analysis underpinning the New Labour project. Its key ideas, synthesised and put forward most influentially by Anthony Giddens (now Lord Giddens), were globalisation and individualisation.[3] Giddens described the transformation of nation states - and the class settlements and welfare regimes which had been negotiated within their boundaries - by global market forces and their attendant flows of capital, commodities, information and people. The essential programmatic idea was adapt, adapt, adapt to this new environment. (This was the main point of Blair's 'education, education, education'.) Hence the agendas of competitiveness, consumer choice and flexibility, and the rejection of Fordist and statist models of production and social provision.

While this position had its moment, in its confrontation with the old state paternalist social democratic legacy, the moment is now passing. Its continued reassertion by New Labour denies the newly emerging realities. The main problem we currently face is the turbulence threatened by global market forces, and by the effects of economic growth, not least environmentally. What is needed is an active state which can address these issues, promote discussion and understanding of them, and enable people to face up to the difficult choices that must now be made.[4] An alliance with neo-conservatives in Washington, and a disciplinary social agenda at home, are not well positioned for the addressing of these problems.

Here then is a looming series of issues. What is not needed is a continuance of the previous New Labour 'project' of marketisation and Americanisation (there are connections between the international and domestic dimensions of the latter). Going on as before, hoping that economic good fortune will continue, is not going to suffice. What is required is to develop a coherent frame of analysis and principles with which to respond to the issues of global market failure, unsustainability, and competing resource claims, which have been put out of mind for too long.

If these are not found, the unprecedented opportunity of a third term in

---

3. Anthony Giddens's books on this topic include *Beyond Left and Right: The Future of Radical Politics* (1994) and *The Third Way: the Renewal of Radical Politics* (1998). For a critique see M. Rustin, 'The Future of Post-Socialism', *Radical Philosophy* 43, 1995.
4. The inadequacies of governmental capacities in the European Union, in the context of its recent enlargement, are now threatening to derail this project. Structures (and budgets) which sufficed for a few member states led by the alliance of France and Germany are failing miserably for an EU of 25 member states.

government will be squandered, as incoherent and opportunistic responses to each issue fragment the government's already weakened constituency. At this point, analysis and deliberation are important, since public opinion needs to be engaged in and prepared for many difficult decisions. These have not been strengths of New Labour's rather frenetic and authoritarian style so far; nor is it clear that the Labour Party any longer possesses much capacity to promote such thought. Unpopular issues need to be faced up to in the first two years of the government's new term, before they rise up to sink it later on. Gordon Brown has throughout presented himself, as Chancellor, as a realist. For this reason he has a better chance than Tony Blair of bringing off such a repositioning, and of maintaining public confidence in the face of difficulties. The sooner, therefore, the transition to a new leadership takes place, the better.

Soundings

is now *freely* available *online* to all subscribers

Benefits include:

♦ Document to document linking using live references, for fast, reliable access to wider, related literature.

♦ Journal content that is fully searchable, across full text, abstracts, titles, TOCs and figures.

♦ Live links to and from major Abstract and Indexing resources to aid research.

♦ The ability to conduct full-text searching across multiple journals, giving you a wider view of the research that counts.

♦ Powerful TOC alerting services that keep you up to date with the latest research.

Set up access now at: www.ingentaselect.com/register.htm
and follow the online instructions*

Subscription Enquiries: help@ingenta.com
*Access is provided by Ingenta Select, an Ingenta website

Pornography now

Stephen Maddison

Pamela Church Gibson (ed), *More Dirty Looks: Gender, Pornography and Power* (2nd Edition), BFI 2004

Do we really need more writing on porn?

On the one hand, the social and economic significance of porn demands that it continue to be the subject of academic and critical engagement. An industry probably more profitable than Hollywood, Nashville or US major league sports, and certainly more productive in terms of sheer volume of output than any other popular cultural form, would seem to necessitate intellectual consideration on a scale similar to that undertaken in relation to music, literature or film. A cultural form that straddles the boundaries between public and private, representation and embodiment, sexual intimacy and corporate power, and which is currently a battleground over questions of surveillance and national security would seem to warrant serious critical reflection. Wouldn't it?

On the other hand, academic and critical engagement with porn has tended to be characterised by a sectarian impasse; and this has been unproductive for a wider demystification of porn (let alone to an informed critical engagement with it), and damaging to the strategic effectiveness of feminism as an urgent political force. For those of us with personal and professional interest in the so-called porn wars, the matrix of skirmishes between anti-porn, pro-censorship, anti-anti-porn, anti-censorship, pro-sex, sex-radical, libertarian, and radical feminist bridgeheads, amongst others, are exhausting and disheartening (not least, as Lynne Segal points out in this collection, because the effort of maintaining a left-radical position amounts to standing still and not saying very much because of the burden of rearticulation). It's little wonder that a terrain once electrified with debate and activism has been eclipsed by the pleasures of commodity fetishism (a point eloquently made by Gibson in the 'shop snapshots' she offers in her preface to this collection).

Okay, so we do need more writing on porn. The questions are then: is *this* the book on porn we need?

How do we write about porn now? How do we write about the most financially substantial of all the branches of the entertainment industry, without taking up a position on one of the pre-existing treadmills of rhetoric? I want to discuss whether these questions are addressed by the second edition of this collection, which in its first incarnation in 1993 was subtitled *Women, Pornography, Power*. The shift from *Women* to *Gender* isn't just titular: the second incarnation (shock, horror) includes essays written by men. The new edition reproduces eight of the original thirteen essays and adds ten new ones; and it also reprints a Lynne Segal essay from 1998 and a Richard Dyer one from 1994 (both of which are available elsewhere). So, the cover price gets you ten new works, and an assortment of ten 'classic' ones. For the sake of space, I'm going to confine my remarks here to some of the 'new' works included, rather than those which appeared in the first collection.

Pamela Church Gibson's preface takes a justificatory stance, and makes a spirited defence of the need for a second collection (although not for reprinting so much stuff from the first one). It's an eloquent and engaged piece of writing, but rather undeveloped, which is a shame - I'd have liked to have read more. The motif of 'shop snapshots', and the identification of key conjunctions - the Countryside Alliance, Stop the War coalition, East Oxford Women's Centre and the sex shop across the street, Silver Moon, the BBFC and Breillat's *Romance*, all of which are deftly positioned in an accessible way - gets the book off to a jolly start. This is followed by a foreword by the ever delicious Henry Jenkins (I'm a fan), who lives up to my hero-worship with a rousing discussion of the problems and rewards of attempting to teach porn as part of the university curriculum. Given the cultural and economic importance of porn (and the level of consumption undertaken by so many of my students), it's a politically unsatisfying irony that there are such problems inherent in organising formal study of it; but there is some consolation in that Jenkins has used this opportunity to prioritise questions of pedagogy and curriculum content rather than theoretical reification. Adulation intact.

After the precise, but undeveloped, set of conjunctions outlined in the introduction, and Jenkins's manifesto, Paul Willeman's densely historicised essay comes at first as an unwelcome shock, demanding as it does such fierce concentration. His specification of the evolution of pornography as a distinct representational form is compelling and persuasive - particularly so for its insistence on tracking the political shifts in Anglo-American culture since the enlightenment. There's something almost louche about the pleasure of intellectualism in his rhetoric as it formulates an agenda that calls for a pornography that refuses 'virtuality', and would thus run counter to 'the prevailing aesthetic' and so 're-emphasise the complexities of "knowing" the other' (p23). This is a discourse on porn that is genuinely post- the porn wars: it has a sensitivity to gender steeped in feminist knowledge, and to porn born of consumption and pleasure. There's a certain dandified libertarianism that informs his desire for a representation of sex capable of facilitating thought unconstrained by market ideologies and the 'Old Corruptions' of religion (p16) (his admission that this is 'mercifully the one and only thought which puts me in the company of the likes of Catherine MacKinnon' (p16) is fabulously arch). But what ultimately makes this essay so delightful is its adroit political sophistication - frankly so often lacking in discussion of porn - and its audacity in attempting to imagine how it might be different. On first reading I found this chapter rather pompous; now I think it's the collection's highlight.

In her chapter, Jane Juffer offers a useful summary of some of the key ideas in her important and thoughtful book *At Home with Pornography*, which is updated to take account of the increasing media awareness of the size and scope of the porn industry. This is a satisfying chapter: given its origins in a substantial and sustained piece of research, there are consistent and coherent arguments and approaches here that throw light on important contexts for understanding women's consumption of pornography in the domestic sphere. Similarly worthwhile, Chuck Kleinhans' essay eschews theoretical precocity and instead makes a persistent, and thoughtful engagement with the pressing cultural, economic and legal issues raised by child porn in the context of the widespread sexualisation of children in US commodity culture. One key strength is that it rehearses important debates not only with reference to specific (horrifying) cases, but to wider economic and social policies. This facilitates an understanding of the forces that shape a terrain characterised by anxiety and emotional exploitation. The essay doesn't offer any surprising or challenging insights, but it is well researched and lucid, and presents the issues in a context that does justice to their urgency. This would make an excellent piece to use in a teaching context.

The significance of Richard Dyer's essay lies not so much in the specific argument he makes (that a sub-genre of gay porn foregrounds the motif of self-reflexivity, and this performativity represents an important component of gay sexuality), but in the fact of his writing in a detailed, serious and unapologetic way about gay porn. Porn has had a particularly important place in gay and pre-gay subcultures, for its candid and affirming portrayal of same-sex intimacy. But queers who have wanted to preserve wide political coalitions have suffered the porn wars in a state of intellectual constipation on this question, since female-identified gender dissent and feminist politics have been critical strategies in the emergence of queer politicisation. First published in 1994, Dyer's piece at the time offered a template for thinking critically about gay porn from the perspective of someone who had actually watched it (and wasn't afraid to show it), and it's fitting that it should be reprinted here alongside contemporary work on gay porn.

Cante and Restivo's essay on the work of Kristen Bjorn, a producer whose work is so distinctive and which has been so well marketed as to constitute a brand identity, unfolds a subtle argument that critiques the eroticisation of national and ethnic difference, yet also reveals a utopian, potentially radical, undercurrent in the films' substitution of 'the brother for the patriarch and the "gang" for the "couple", and the future for the past' (p124). Mahawatte's essay on gay Arab fetishism in online newsgroups and solo movies offers an intriguing interpretation of the conjunction of sexualised anti-Islamic news coverage of the fall of the Taliban in Kandahar, and J.A. Boone's analysis of the homoerotics of sexology and anthropology. I found this essay stimulating, and lamented that it wasn't longer.

In conjunction with the rest of the reprinted essays (and given that you get almost twice as much material in the second edition), this collection definitely ranks as essential for anyone interested in the field. My wish list for the third edition would include Gibson herself contributing an essay (and not just the Preface), Lynne Segal writing about something other than Catherine MacKinnon, and more Willeman, Juffer and Jenkins.

Life after meaning

Caroline Bassett

Tiziana Terranova, *Network Culture: Politics for an Information Age*
Pluto, 2004

Network Culture is a book exploring aspects of digital culture and digital history, ranging across biotech, copyright/copyleft, the political economy of the media industries and the constitution of new forms of collective life. All of these are re-examined through the lenses of first and second wave cybernetics, and various other forms of information science. Terranova argues that new political possibilities emerge in an age when cultural processes take on 'the attributes of information' (p7), and when the dynamics of the natural and social world are re-thought in informational terms. Indeed, information means that the assumed divisions between the categories of nature and culture have themselves to be re-considered. Given all this, radical social construction as a way of thinking about techno-culture misses the point: some other approach is needed (p121).

It is important to grasp at the outset that Terranova is not exactly attempting an informational-scientific reading of culture. Rather, she is exploring what she terms the *corollaries* she finds between physical descriptions of information and informational culture. These corollaries underpin the account of contemporary culture developed here, an account characterised by a fierce insistence on the productive force of information. This productivity is explored not only in relation to information's *creative*, as well as its *destructive*, potential, but also in relation to the questions of predictability and control (and their limits) that are raised by cybernetics, information theory, and later AL (artificial life) and cellular automata.

The nub of the argument is that, alongside its obvious capacity to order cultural formations (quantifying, and in this sense reducing everyday life to pre-plotted probability), information has the capacity to produce the surprising, the improbable, the *virtual*. It is characteristic of the sudden leaps that both electrify and problematise this book that the virtual here is defined - in philosophical (Bergsonian) rather than technical terms - as the *unexpected*. These irruptions of the virtual (these unexpected emergences) are here understood as intrinsic to information and to informational culture; which is, after all, widely characterised by abundance and redundancy as well as command and control. Terranova argues that new forms of political organisation may cohere around these irruptions, which might also constitute the grounds for a new form of politics (p154), one which can take a 'stab at the fabric of possibility' by un-doing 'the coincidence of the real with the given' (p27).

The distinction between this approach and forms of utopian politics based on imaginative projection (ways of 'thinking the future differently' as Braidotti once put it) is usefully drawn here, not least because the latter was much drawn on in late 1990s writing on cyberspace. For Terranova a politics can be founded on the exploitation of *realised* shifts or rents in the fabric of the given. She is interested, for instance, in the consequences of the fact that through the productive re-orderings of networks, an improbable possibility briefly flashed into being: the free net, the cyborg citizen, the electronic commons all really existed. For her, however, the point isn't that these developments generated new utopian possibilities for the future; nor is it that what is momentarily 'decoded, freed up' is almost at the same time re-coded or co-opted (p118) - although, as she rightly observes, this does happen. The key is that reality *swerved*. As they said in *The Matrix* when the cat walked by twice: something changed in the system.

In *Network Culture* there are two major (and connected) focuses through which these ideas are explored and developed, and through which specific corollaries between information science and cultural formations are made. The first of these is the informational environment or *milieu* that increasingly constitutes our cultural horizons.

Here the launch point is the tensioned relationship between communication, defined as message, and information, defined through its affective properties as something that exceeds the message, and certainly exceeds meaning - and thereby confounds the narrow boundaries of the sender/ receiver model, instead bringing into being an environment.

The relationship between information and communication, sketched out in fairly abstract ways in the early chapters, is explored in more detail later in the book, including in the section on communications, where it is used to explore distinctions between communication management strategists (awarded ownership of 'technical conceptions' of communications) and journalists operating with a traditional journalistic code of ethics. This case study is intriguing. It also leaves some questions unanswered - not least because it tends to ignore the affective punch of news journalism (its narrative aspect, in a sense). There is surely more to the opposition between the operations of these two groups than the existence on the one side of truth, honour and rational debate, and on the other the infinitely transferable and infinitely empty Nike swoosh-meme? It isn't an accident, perhaps, that it is in relation to *specific* cultural forms (in this case the news economy), that information science/ informational culture corollaries become harder to use; or rather, that they seem to offer less. One way around these limitations, of course, is to utilise a range of information science accounts, deploying them as necessary; certainly Terranova herself - more or less mid-stream - changes the corollary 'source code' from an (information theory) account based on the linear system of message and receiver to (cybernetic) accounts of feedback, avowedly to get around what would otherwise look embarrassingly like an acceptance of behaviourism in her own account of reception and/in the kinds of informational milieu she describes.

The meditation on information as communication's excess explored above is paralleled by the treatment Terranova accords to the question of the relationship between the mass and the multitude, so that a discussion of biopower becomes a meditation on the changes in state that switch the mass (characterised by passivity) into the multitude (characterised by its demanding clamour, its *demand* for spectacle), and *vice versa*. Here the mark of Hardt and Negri's *Empire* is very clear - and so is the Foucault-inspired desire to erase the subject. Indeed, if the multitude is the new collective, the individual is almost entirely absent from Terranova's account. Her sense is that informational culture works with pre-individual units (and here parallels are made with Dawkin's selfish gene, and arguments about the gene as the level at which natural selection operates), and with collective units, but not with the category of the individual subject (reduced, as Foucault had it, from model to tool, as she notes). Chapters on soft control, drawing on cellular automata and artificial life, develop these ideas in relation to social phenomena such as 'closed' reality TV shows, where control is exercised only at particular points (when decanting and incarcerating contestants, for instance).

Terranova is to be applauded for the scope and ambition of her bid to think through the contemporary connections between cybernetics and information theory and cultural form. It is also clear that this does yield some surprising and suggestive results - sudden moments of epiphany where a particular dynamics is revealed through its 'informational' description.

However there are some issues here. At times the attempt to find corollaries collapses, and the reader is left with a connection sustained only by rhetoric or metaphor - even while something rather more substantial is implied. More rarely, there are passages where the reader senses an absolute lack of connection; of a broken link between two forms of thinking.

The belief that developments in information science - and particularly in information systems - can be used to offer insights into cultural forms, particularly the cultural forms, out of which these developments come, is of course long-standing. Cybernetics in particular always had colonising ambitions, as excellent accounts of the early Macy conferences on cybernetics show. It is also true that Norbert Wiener himself, the father of cybernetics (proverbially at least), always had doubts about the degree to which cybernetics could map the social world, believing that problems of scale would emerge. As he put it: 'we are too small to influence the stars … too large to care about anything but the mass effects of molecules'.[1] Perhaps his objections still stand today. They are, at any rate, at the root of my own unease with Terranova's negotiation of this connection. The quality of the relays 'between the technical and social' that she describes seem arbitrarily erected at times - veering between instantiation and recourse to the concealed absolutism of the metaphorical (chaos is chaos theory, is social chaos). To put it as Haraway didn't: there's a code trick here.

---

1. Norbert Wiener, *Cybernetics, or control and communication in the animal and the machine*, MIT 1961, p163.

Finally, I note that others in media studies looking at the informational milieu, have been down roads rather like this before. Stuart Hall himself developed encoding/decoding more or less in response to (or rather in revolt from) cybernetic models of communication. His turn from code into language, indeed, might be said to mirror Terranova's contemporary turn from language to information (see p10).

Setting these issues aside, what is clear is that Terranova's account demonstrates the extraordinarily *suggestive* power of the 'new science' to explain the contemporary world; to re-assess the relationship 'between culture, power and information', as she puts it. This suggestive power is here deployed to great effect, and is above all used to explore the multitude as a political concept within an informational milieu. Perhaps this emphasis emerges because Tiziana Terranova has the soul of an activist. More Negri than Hardt, and beyond (and through) questions of the philosophical and epistemological status of science, it is actually the old question of 'what is to be done?' that she addresses. The sense of information's possibility she describes is light years away from the kind of celebratory rhetoric of 'revolution-achieved' characteristic of much early cyberspace writing. If the communications channel thickens to become information space, if the inert mass transforms into the dynamic and demanding multitude operating beyond absolute spectacularisation, and beyond the degree zero of the political (if the multitude comes to a kind of life *after* meaning we could say), then for Terranova this constitutes the *grounds* for a meaningful politics to begin. As she puts it, there is 'nothing idyllic' to be found here. I don't always agree with her arguments, but I want to be on her side.

Poems

Travelling

I
We walk to the shrine of the diamond-eyed god
This is the hour he's in green and gold
The women moan

He looks a little camp to me
upturned palm with rose
joss sticks burning

but oh those black granite thighs

II
Green roses on a terrace
lemon grass, a golden moon
a golden oriole chases a crow

Mine host waxeth sentimental.
Not a lover in sight.

III
The tattered balladeers invoke the
sun, the moon, the stars,
sing of kings who rode a night of sand
to plant a flag
on yet another sand dune,
of women who died when the sands shifted
in the wind.
A bulbul sings in the thorn tree.

IV
Wedged between houses, a sliver of sea,
casuarinas, clean sand,
infinity.

V
This town boasts a one-armed postal clerk
always drunk
a dog named Dumpy who can't stand the smell of drink
a street with three war widows and two light-eyed girls
who went astray
seven hen-pecked husbands
Copernicus who likes to treat his friends
and disappear when the bill appears...

Never underestimate a dishevelled town
the Colonel says
reaching for the rum.

Eunice de Souza

Lilac in the rain
for Bill Upchurch, May 2005

The lilac spreads as if the weight of air
  were something it had to accommodate.
    Its frailest branches are laden with bloom
      so the flowers point downward in the rain.

    Last night there was thunder and the skylight pane
      snapped and popped echoing through the room
  along with the thunder in crisp, separate
hammer taps and all the flowers were bare

to the elements, beaten down but still rich
  in their range of pinks, dowsed in shades
    of fragility, in the dark, under flashes of light
      while we slept and woke and slept again till now

    it is difficult to understand just how
      the rules of sleep work or how the lilac might
  survive such beatings or how dreams fade
into objects so we can't tell which is which.

George Szirtes

Someone who dies in a vision

from the Chinese of Yang Lian, with a nod to Brian Holton
(inspired by the book by Yeats)

someone who dies in a vision   is like a poet who dies in a poem
summer enters your tower and ascends
you contemplate like a god, rave like a god
number flocks of swans obsessively per millennium   amend
the moon   that order bleeding from thin dark claws
puts a rat through its paces with ingenuity
you grow weary of it all   even for the wise, dying is still death
but writing   that twice-lost stony art
reeks of rot as it gnaws your flesh
you leap into the flames again   like a work discarded

so   we die in you
the only inheritance a marble chair
your seat amid the keening of the blind
one man's feet   trampling innocent grapes
a vision   you said   that is to imitate ghosts in order to live
to make inquiries   like an old beggar
corpsed on the street   mourned by the incarnadine teeth of savage cats
but a rose smelted out of a poem, now   that shock will always cause wonder

Yang Lian
Translated by Seán Golden

Keane

After Heaney

And sometime take the Central Line out east
to follow a hedgerow along Luxborough Lane
till you reach a training ground and field,
where players strike like October wind,

and a squad, divided like a cell developing,
shoots at shifted goalposts at close range,
so that you catch an Ireland international
getting past an England keeper's defence,

and as he leaves his signature, eyes
the colour of the ocean off County Clare
blow your heart, till you are leagues away
on the rock of another age and shore.

Sarah Wardle

The trees outside my window

after Jules Supervielle

I'm thankful to the trees outside my window.
Only they can reach into the depths of me.
Without them, I should have died long ago -
they keep my heart alive, its eager ways.

In the long willow branches, the dark cypress
my own ghost hides, stares out at me,
knowing me so well, pitying me in this world.
So little understanding why I stay and stay.

Moniza Alvi

Institutions and racism

Equality in the workplace
Farhad Dalal

Farhad Dalal *argues that ideas of racism and racial equality are embedded in processes of group formation and belonging. Understanding these processes may help us to make practices of racialisation more visible.*

Individuals, groups and racial groups

The word 'race' is a commonplace. It is readily overheard in conversations at bus stops and dinner tables; it is cited frequently in newspaper columns as they describe the goings on in the world; politicians and activists continually draw on the idea of race; there are entire academic journals and departments dedicated to its study. And perhaps most importantly, the term is enshrined in British law through the Race Relations Act (1976) and its amendments. By virtue of the fact that the term 'race' is granted legal status, we are all *obliged* to engage with it. If we do not, 'the law' will reprimand and chastise us variously. Peculiarly, however, the groupings that *race* relations regulations require organisations to monitor are not *racial* categories but *ethnic* ones. Why is this and what is the difference between them?

It is impossible to find definitions of race that are meaningfully distinguishable from those of ethnicity and culture. In their advice to the citizens of this country, the CRE rely on Suman Fernando's definitions of these terms: *race* - to do with visible physical appearance, said to be determined by genetic ancestry; *culture* - beliefs and behaviours shared by the group, said to be determined by education, upbringing and choice; and *ethnicity* - shared history, language, culture, a group identity defined from within, which is said to be determined by group identity, social pressure, and the need to belong. There are a great many problems with this way of dividing up the world. For example, the definitions overlap with each other (culture is made part of the definition of ethnicity); they are tautological (ethnicity is defined as a group identity the cause of which is group identity); although race is defined as having to do with physical differences, it is agreed by Fernando himself that there are no such things as races. Similar difficulties are to be found in all definitions that seek to differentiate this trinity.

In fact, it is accepted generally within many discourses (for instance biology and sociology) that there are no such things as races *per se*. If one accepts this, as I do, then we are faced with a critical problem: if there are no such things as 'races', how can there be a thing called 'racism'? Surely racism exists - but what does it consist of?

The legislation tries to get around the problem by making a distinction between racism and discrimination (on the basis of a - false - dichotomy between thought and action), and then limiting itself to the latter. Racism is said to be the *belief* that some races are superior to others, whilst discrimination is to do with the *activity* of treating people 'less favourably on grounds of their colour, race, nationality or national or ethnic origin'. Race Relations legislation allegedly limits itself to what people do, and does not address what they think. (In its literature the CRE appears to take race itself as a taken-for-granted category.)

The House of Lords sought to clarify the definition of a racial group as that which has a long shared history and a cultural tradition of its own.[1] These two factors are said to be *essential* to the demarcation of a racial group. Also relevant (but not necessary) requirements are having a common geographical origin, as well as a common language, literature and religion. But surely these latter are categories of culture as they are usually understood. And what of this idea of 'origin'? In which epoch of the continuing nomadic history of the human species (which as far as we know walked out of Africa) are we going to draw a line, take

---

1. In 1983: see www.cre.gov.uk/gdpract/ed_s_legal.html.

a snapshot, and say that this is where people are 'originally' from? Interestingly, the House of Lords make no mention of physical characteristics in their clarifications of race. So is a racial grouping the same as that of culture?

In fact, when the *activity* of racial discrimination is defined, the physical characteristic of colour does feature. Discrimination is said to be *racial* if it takes place on the grounds of colour, nationality, race, ethnic or national origin. A history of the terms race, culture and ethnicity shows three things. First, a mish-mash of very different *types* of things are used to define them - nationality, geography, religion, language, behaviours, beliefs, some notion of 'where people are originally from', and colour. Second, whilst attempts to define the terms continually collapse into each other, the notion of colour (in particular those of black and white) has been used from the very beginning to name all three - we talk readily of white and black races, cultures and ethnic groups. Third, there is no agreement as to the number of races or cultures or ethnicities; they seem to spring up suddenly in contexts in which they were previously invisible.

This invites a shift of focus from what these terms actually are to the *functions* they serve. I suggest that the terms are evoked at particular times and places in order to *create* distinctions, so as to be able to differentiate the 'haves' from the 'must-not-haves'; in brief, in order to create an 'us' and a 'them'. Thus what is critical is not racism, but racialisation, by which I mean the *activity* which consists of the evocation of the mythic idea of race as an explanatory or organising principle. Thus racism is not just a belief, it is first and foremost an activity.

The question that should continually be asked is thus the reasons for any of these terms being used at a particular moment and in a particular time: who is seeking to make a differentiation and for what reason?

The language used to describe Africans and other exotics (lascivious monstrous types, apelike, and so on) in the travel records of the early European adventurers is language we would clearly call racist in today's terms. Yet they did not make use of the term race in their descriptions. I think that this is because at that time the African was not yet human, and so was already Other. Over time, accumulating evidence forces one to admit Africans into the body of humanity, and this is the moment when the term race is required to keep them Other. It is now admitted that whilst they are human, they are of a different race. When the category of race started to crumble in the early twentieth century, then culture came to the fore. Now, it is said that while we might all be one race, they are of a different culture. As the idea of cultural difference becomes difficult to sustain in any meaningful way, there is a retreat to the idea of ethnicity - the internal sense of belonging to a group. The term ethnicity has more respectability, but its work is no different from that of race. The fact that *race* relations legislation requires one to monitor *ethnic* groups is testament to that fact.

It is also the case that a semantic history of the terms black and white in the English language shows that the associations and meanings of the terms have

'we need a shift of focus from what these terms actually are to the functions they serve'

not been there 'naturally' from the beginning, but have developed and grown over the last five hundred years or so into the signifiers of negativity and positivity that we come to take for granted today. In the English language the terms start off more or less neutrally. From the Middle Ages

onwards, white comes progressively to be associated with goodness and positivity, and black with badness and negativity. (For example, blackness does not become associated with death until the fourteenth century.) Eventually (from the eighteenth century onwards), they come even to name things that can have no colour - the emotions - in order to signal where they are positioned on the scale of approval - for example 'black anger'. I would argue that notions of black and white are critical to the project of racialising the world, and that they have been honed to work as signifiers of exclusion and inclusion. It is no coincidence that the Black was named as such by those that designated themselves as Whites. And it is no coincidence that the association and uses of the words mushroomed during the European Imperial adventures beginning in the seventeenth century. It is because race is an empty category that it has had to increasingly rely on an idea of colour to sustain differentiations. Thus the world is colour coded because it has been racialised.

Another part of the argument is that, as each of us is born into, and goes through the psycho-social developmental processes in an already racialised and colour coded world, we inevitably imbibe the discourses with our mother's milk. So it is that our psyches too are inevitably racialised and colour coded, so much so that it becomes 'natural' in day to day speech to reach for the word 'black' when one wants to signal disapproval in some way. A trivial example:

the fish caught illicitly and sold clandestinely during the fishing crisis of 1995 were spontaneously called 'black fish' on the BBC news (BBC1, *Nine O'clock News*, 12.2.95).

In sum, the so-called racial identities are fictions manufactured by colonising processes. The fact that they come to be taken up as essentialist categories by those that the categories sought to marginalise speaks not to their reality, but to the power of ideology and discourses that we cannot help but imbibe through the psycho-social developmental processes we are bound to go through.

But saying that 'races' are fictions and reifications does not provide solutions to the problem of racism. The paradox is that something that has no material existence comes nonetheless to have a very powerful experiential and psychological existence, so much so that it has a critical role in the manufacture of individual identities. The fact that the world and the discourses have been racialised and colour coded means that we not only come to experience the world in racialised ways: we continually reproduce and reinforce the racialisations in our interactions with each other.

Despite the problems with the word ethnicity, it does capture something significant in its gesture towards the notion of belonging. Radical Group Analytic Theory (based on the work of the group analyst S.H. Foulkes and the sociologist Norbert Elias) would concur with the view that the need to belong is intrinsic and essential to the human condition. However, belonging is not a straightforward experience - it is a problematic. It is impossible to say just what is the essence of a particular 'us', say Britishness. When we look directly at the British 'us', we find not homogeneity but diversity - multiple groupings, overlapping and conflictual: vegetarians, landlords, Scots, accountants, miners, Christians, Muslims, fascists, liberals, and so on. And if one turns one's attention to each of these sub-groupings, they too disintegrate into further arrays of diversity. It is precisely because of the impossibility of finding and naming the essence of the 'us' that one looks to the margins to the 'not-us', and uses colour to demarcate them. However, the idea of the 'not-us' is beset by the same set of problems as the 'us', in that there is no unity to be found there either. Nevertheless, our minds somehow manage this feat of registering, in any particular moment, an experience of an 'us' that is contrasted with a 'them': a difference not of degree, but of type. Here is the conundrum: I can always say that two things are the *same* by virtue of one attribute (say redness) and *different* by virtue of another (say age). *Both are simultaneously true.* So the question then becomes *why in some circumstances do I find myself having an experience of similarity, and in other circumstances I find myself fixated by the differences.*

As the question is such an important one, let me ask it again in a slightly different form: out of the infinity of differences between any two people, why does one of these differences come to be more meaningful than the rest? The same can be, and needs to be, asked of similarities.

To talk about belonging is to talk of a sense of an 'us'. But the logic of belonging is paradoxical. For the notion of belonging to have any rational or emotional meaning and significance, two conditions of necessity must be fulfilled. First, in order to be able to belong to one place, it is necessary for there to be another place that one does *not* belong to. Second, there must be some who are decreed *not* to be part of the belonging group. If either of these conditions are not fulfilled, then the territory of belonging would become infinitely big and encompass everyone, and so become meaningless. This then is the hard truth about 'belonging' - it is created by and through the mechanisms of inclusion and exclusion to which the notion of power relations is critical.

The multiculturalist response

Words are indeed very powerful things. They are so powerful that their mere use not only leads us to believe that the thing they refer to exists; it also leads us *to act and behave* in ways that take account of the things that are being alluded to. Thus the attempts to deal with racism that accept the idea of race are bound to create new difficulties and conundrums. One significant attempt is multiculturalism.

The watchword of multiculturalism is 'equal but different'. In this world view, because they do not understand each other's belief systems, when people of different cultures, ethnicities or races, etc, encounter each other, they are inclined to misinterpret what they encounter; and this in turn arouses in them a mixture of anxiety and hostility. The solution proposed is a mixture of education and tolerance: education, in terms of learning about the Other culture and making it familiar; and tolerance, in terms of tolerating something that is causing one some kind of discomfort. This strategy, although completely sensible in one regard, avoids confronting the problematic of *power* and renders the world more benign than it actually is.

One of the ways of testing the multiculturalist thesis is by asking the question, when is an encounter between two (or more) people thought to be *not* multicultural? Consider: the very notion of multicultural suggests the possibility of its normative inverse, something which one might call mono-cultural. Similarly, the affiliated idea of a 'cross-cultural' encounter implies the possibility of an encounter that remains within the tram lines of a mono-culture. But, as I have been arguing, there can be no such thing as a mono-culture. Cultures are structures that institutionalise power relationships. What's more, the notion of a transcultural encounter is also problematic, as it invokes an idea of an encounter taking place in a region in some way beyond, outside, or prior to, culture itself. Let me put it this way: why do we tend to call the encounter between Mr Singh and Mr Smith multi or cross cultural, and not the encounter between Mr Smith and Mr Jones?

There are two dangers here. One is *culturalism*, in which we become fixated by culture; the other is trying to do away with culture entirely, to end up in a *culture-free* space. These dangers are founded on, and alternate between, two kinds of errors. The first error is to take the division of humanity into cultures, races or ethnicities as unproblematic givens, so that the issue becomes one of 'how to negotiate these differences': culturalism is the tendency to get mesmerized by some of the divisions between human groupings found in the *external* social world. The alternative position, of a culture-free space, assumes that there can be a retreat into the *internal* world of individuals, and that human nature, our humanity, is something outside or prior to the social. My argument - in contrast to both these positions - is that these categories do not exist out there in nature: they are generated and sustained by the logic of power relations.

Institutional racism and the workplace

For the purposes of this analysis, let us say that racism is a mechanism that works against the principle of equality. What I want to turn to now are the workings of racism in the workplace. The first thing to be said is that the workings of racism are usually invisible. In all countries, it so happens that certain groupings tend to do less well in the job market. It is not even clear that there is a problem here. Two or more people went for an interview and one of them got the job. In such circumstances, the conclusion one is often forced to draw is that the world as we find it (these people here better off, and those people there not so well off) is because some kinds of people are just better at some kinds of tasks. (In Finland for example, a country justly proud of its social conscience and democratic practices, about 55 per cent of graduates are women; and the majority of those getting higher grades are also women. Yet when it comes to managers in organisations at the highest levels, women make up just 6 per cent of them.)

So something more must be going on in such situations, something that the principle of equal opportunities does not solve. When that something is clearly colour coded, it is called *institutional racism* (now renamed 'indirect racial discrimination' in the legislation).

I must say that for a long time I struggled to really know quite what was being talked about when the term institutional racism was used. How can an institution *do* anything? Because ultimately an institution only consists of the individuals that belong to it. And I have created a further problem through the way I have been talking about racism. I have reified 'racism' by saying things like 'the work of racism', and so made racism sound like it is a thing - a thing that does things to us. It then appears that racism itself is the problem. It is not. The problem is the way that human beings find themselves experiencing and treating other human beings.

How power is institutionalised

I was recently helped to understand the term institutional racism through the story of a school teacher. The teacher really struggled to maintain discipline in his first year of teaching. One day early on in his second year he was excited to have found a solution for himself. At the very start of the new teaching year with a new class, he presented to the pupils a written set of rules of what was to be not allowed and also a graded set of punishments (detentions and so forth) to do with each infringement. Now when a student misbehaved, he said to them: I am obliged to punish you in this way for this misdemeanour *because it says so in the rules*. The teacher was very excited by the outcome. Wonderfully, the students did not complain but co-operated in the punishment process, because now, whatever was happening, it appeared that it was not the teacher doing it to them. The teacher was only following the same set of rules as the students. The rules had been institutionalised and all were subjugated by them.

The world is not as simple as this classroom, and even the classroom is not as simple as I have portrayed it. However, the very simplicity of the story allows us to see some of the elements of institutionalisation that are normally invisible. Specifically, although on the one hand it is clear that it is the teacher who has actually created the rules, in day to day practice it appears that the teacher is powerless to do otherwise than he does; he is obliged to follow the rules like everyone else.

The point is made clearer through another trivial experience. Recently, whilst walking along a road I saw a shortish policeman. It occurred to me that this was another example of the institutionalising mechanisms at work. In the past, when the rules said that the minimum height for policemen was to be six foot (or whatever it was) then this rule 'naturally' excluded people from certain parts of the world from becoming policemen. There was no single person, no grand conspiracy, no statute in Home Office regulations saying that (say) Tamils should not be policemen - it is just an unfortunate outcome of a rule that all are subject to. Of course there are always rationales for the rules, rationales that seek to explain the necessity of the rule being the way it is. However, these *rationales* are not as *rational* as they might initially appear. In actual fact all *rationales* must always contain within them some element of *rationalisation*.

One can see clearly in the first story that the schoolteacher had the power to determine what the rules were. However, we can also see that in the practical situation in the classroom, that fact has become invisible to the school children. We can intuit that some years later the way in which these rules came into being will have been completely forgotten. This would give us the impression of the rules having always been there - from the beginnings of time. This is the process of institutionalisation. Further, we can see that the process of institutionalisation obscures the workings of power, leaving us with the illusion that the situation we are faced with is natural, self-evident, and eternal. It then appears to us that policemen just *are* tall, and it does not even occur to us to question the hows, whys and wherefores of the situation.

This description I have given of the processes of institutionalisation is exactly how ideology is usually described. As is well known, the function of ideology is to give particular historical and contingent arrangements of the world the impression of necessity and inevitability. As Roland Barthes put it, ideology transforms history into nature. Thus I would say that the processes of institutionalisation are identical to the workings of ideology, and indeed each is an aspect of the other.

The thing about power is that the more one has, the more one is able to keep up the illusion of having clean hands, of being innocent if you will. For example, the structure of the military is such that the general - having ordered his troops into action - can sit having a quiet evening meal, whilst the dirty of work of killing is being done by others elsewhere. But even though the soldiers are doing the dirty work, the structure of the situation is such that even they need not feel any personal responsibility for the consequences of their actions. This is possible because a function of bureaucratic structures (and hierarchy in general) is to dissipate responsibilities so that it appears that no actual individuals are responsible for what is taking place. The general has the possibility of sleeping with an easy conscience because (a) he is not doing the actual dirty work, and (b) he has given this order in the service of something greater than him - his country, his people and so on - and so can actually feel virtuous and noble whilst other human beings are being slaughtered. Meanwhile the soldier has the possibility of easing his conscience by virtue of the fact that he is only following orders. He can think that as the intention and decision to propel him into action came from elsewhere, that is where ultimate responsibility must lie. There are two caveats I need to make, however. First, I would like to stress that these are possibilities not certainties; guilt and responsibility are never machined away in their entirety - many a soldier and even generals end up traumatised. The second caveat is to say that I am not arguing that one should do away with organisational hierarchies, structures and bureaucracies (which is an impossibility), nor that the primary purpose of these systems is to machine away responsibility (and therefore guilt). I am suggesting that there is something intrinsic to the nature of hierarchical structures that allows them to be used in this way.

We can also get to see in this scenario how rationales are being mobilised to bolster activities. Like the schoolteacher, each can claim that they are only following the rules. It should be stressed, again, that on the whole these rules are experienced as naturally occurring injunctions - to love one's country, to defend one's way of life, and so on.

The analogy of the army also helps us see why it is that the rawest and crudest instances of racism - that is, the most *visible* - are often seen in the most deprived areas. The captains of industry, or you and me sitting having a cappuccino in Covent Garden, are able, just like the generals, to make it appear that our hands are cleaner than they actually are.

The analogy of the classroom, although useful, of course seriously misrepresents the ways in which such rules arise. In the classroom the teacher made a conscious decision to invent the rules in order to manipulate the students. In real life there is no such Machiavellian figure, or international conspiracy, planning how to benefit certain groupings and disenfranchise others. This is a problem which arises in evolutionary theory: how do we end up with things that look like intricate designs despite there being no designer? And the answer in this sociological and psychological arena is the same as in the biological one. These rules emerge and are thrown up by the processes of interaction which take place in the field of power relations. However it is that these rules come about, they inform the shapes and forms that institutions come to take. The result is that institutions, including the workplace, come to embody and represent these self-same rules. In sum, one of the functions of the structure of institutions is to bolster, conserve and perpetuate particular ideologies - and here is the twist: to do so without giving the appearance of doing so.

In the descriptions I have given so far, I have made things appear more fixed and simple than they actually are. Let me correct that now. Institutions, like cultures, are not homogenous in the sense of sustaining a single ideology. In any one moment there are any number of ideologies, in all sorts of shapes and guises, contesting and struggling against each other. One rule might be - we must make money for our shareholders; another rule might be - we must look after our workers; another might be - we must concern ourselves with the environment, and so on.

For ideology to function at its best, it must remain invisible; it must be as though it simply was not there. The reasons, the rationales, for acting in certain ways and not others, must be given a basis in something else, something rational. Although there is always something reasonable in the rational, its very reasonableness serves as a screen that hides the rationalisation.

This invisibility is one reason why the issue of institutional racism is so intractable, and allows numerous commentators to say with equanimity and conviction that there is no such thing as institutional racism - and they say this despite the evidence supplied by an enormous number of reports by government and academic research bodies.

The invisibility of discrimination

Since institutions (no less than individuals) emerge from and reside within psycho-social discourses, they will of necessity come to embody, reproduce and reinforce the prevailing ideologies and conventions that are found there. I take it as axiomatic that one of these conventions is the powerful linkage of blackness with badness, and goodness with whiteness. So all of us, all institutions, must embody and reproduce them in some way.

I would like to stress the phrase 'in some way': this embodiment and reproduction is not the same everywhere and for all people. It is continually contested and modified. So I am not espousing a crude pessimistic determinism in which things are fixed forever. The point is that something exists in the British context (the theme of black and white) that *necessitates* contestation. Thus all institutions will come to have structures that somehow work in the direction of privileging its white constituents over its black ones. Thus there is much evidence that black members of an institution are found to do less well than the white members *at a statistical level*. But because the mechanisms of marginalisation are invisible, there exists the possibility of explaining away these facts in a variety of ways, and it is to these I will now turn.

The denial of the existence of racism is integral to racism itself. It is part of what makes it work. If there is no problem in the first place, then nothing needs to be done. The understandings that are offered to explain why things are happening in the way that they are, are rationalisations masquerading as explanations, whose function it is to *explain away* the possibility of something untoward happening at an institutional level.

The first kind of *explanation* is the idea that if the white members are doing better in the system, then it is because they *are* better. The rationale behind this explanation is that of meritocracy. And this must indeed be true on some occasions - at times a white colleague is more deserving of promotion than a black colleague. The key here is the phrase 'some occasions', because on other occasions this is not the case. But the way things work, the instances in which the assertion is true are used to make invisible the occasions on which it is not true. And the way in which this happens is as follows.

It is the nature of statistical evidence that some of the data that constitute that evidence will directly contradict the statistical truth. For example, a statistical truth might be 'most of the apples in this basket are red'. However, it is also true that *some* of the apples in this same basket are green. What takes place next is that these particular truths are used to deny the veracity of the statistical truth, which is like saying the fact that because *some* of the apples are green must mean that it is not true that most of the apples in the basket are red. For example, it is true that some black lawyers have reached the highest echelons of their profession and become Queens Council. This then is used to make the problem one of particular individuals. It is said if Winston and Satish are able to become QCs, then the fact that Harish, Meena and Sandra have not been able to must have to do with some difficulty *in* them. This then is one of the main strategies used to render institutional racism invisible. What is being said is that institutional racism does not exist, and that the problem as such is that of *particular individuals*.

On some occasions, when it becomes blatantly clear that something racialised has indeed taken place, the individualising strategy is once again called upon to do its work. Now it is the 'bad apple' theory, and it is used to say that it is this or that particular policeman, or social worker, or whoever, who is unfortunately racist. And if we cast out these individuals, things will be ok.

The interplay between visibility and invisibility is a complex one. The question one always needs to attend to is when do people of colour become invisible and when visible? The following story draws out some of the intricacies. Recently I was invited to contribute to a training programme to do with leadership that was designed specifically for the so called ethnic minority members of a number of organisations. By now it is clear what is meant by ethnic minority - black people, the darkies. Anyway, I arrived at lunch time and there in the dining room of this conference centre were two groups having lunch - and it was very clear which was the group I was going to be engaging with. One table was entirely white, and the other primarily black.

I was told by one of the organisers (both white) that those at the white table were here for stage two of the main training. It had been previously noticed by the organisers that participation by the ethnic minority members was almost non-existent in the main training. It had therefore been decided to run one specifically for the ethnic minorities, and so here they were, attending stage one of the same training. Now this seemed to me to be a good thing - they had noticed the problem and tried to do something about it.

During the training session I described the powerful impact the dining room had on me when I first entered it, seeing that the people at one table were all black and the other almost all white. And I had wondered how it was that such a powerful division had come about in that way given that we were not living under a system of apartheid.

Part of the answer was given then by one of the black members who said that on arriving on this course he was surprised to see a white colleague from his organisation in the other training. He was doubly surprised because he did not know (a) that the colleague, whom he thought he knew quite well, was on an *ongoing* training, and (b) he did not even know about the existence of that training. And then he was further surprised to discover two more white colleagues from his organisation also on that training.

How are we to understand what is going on? Clearly something very powerful had gone on in the organisation so that the lines of communication had circumnavigated this person, or gone through him as though he were not there. He was invisible to those who had disseminated information regarding the training. We may surmise that unconsciously - or perhaps consciously - the disseminators discounted him as a potential candidate for that training.

We may surmise further that on his return, if he were to question how and why he was rendered invisible, it is very likely that it would be explained away as a one-off, that it was an oversight of some kind and that it was not done intentionally by anyone. And no doubt this rendition would at some level be true - no one individual intentionally excluded him. There must have been a chain of communication of A telling B about the training, who made a passing reference about it to C at the photocopy machine, and so on. And somehow, this chain never included the black person in question. It is really hard to comprehend how this can happen given that (a) there was no conspiracy, and (b) any one of the people who knew could have linked him into the information chain. This is exactly what makes the process of institutionalisation such a powerful and efficient mechanism in perpetuating ideologies, privileges and divisions. Its very silence and apparent non-existence is its strength.

In my experience, what often happens next is that if the black person persists and does not buy into the one-off explanation, they are seen as difficult and as having a chip on their shoulder. When one does not feel heard, one either gives up, or is compelled to shout louder and louder, until one's voice gets shrill in its insistence, and gets to sound like whining. And *that* certainly does get heard, and is used to condemn the character of the complainer as weak in some way, which in turn distracts from the content of the actual complaint.

Alternatively, the voice might become angry. Now the black person is experienced as threatening and disruptive. One of the defences put up by the institution (more precisely: people who constitute the institution) is one in which it is said that there is no basis in reality for the complaint; there is no conspiracy to keep black people down; the event that took place is a one-off and so meaningless. If this were true then the conclusion that one is then forced to draw is that the difficulties must lie *within* the black person. The protestor becomes perceived as the problem. In effect, what has taken place is that the black person has been diagnosed as being paranoid. The thing to note in these not improbable scenarios is the fact that what has become painfully visible is the black person as bad (angry), mad (paranoid) or weak (whining), and what remains invisible is that which has set off the whole situation in the first place.

There is another lesson to be learnt from this scenario. The fact that a 'special' training was offered to the ethnic minorities can be construed as positive discrimination. This special training is a compensation for a failure within the system. However, if this failure is kept invisible, then the only thing that is visible is apparently that '*they* are getting special treatment! *They* are being favoured over *us!*' We can see then that if the 'compensation' is the only thing that is registered or noticed, it can set off feelings of resentment, jealousy and envy in the mainstream population. Reports in the mainstream media tend to pick up on and report exactly these sorts of 'favours', which in turn inflame the populist mind.

This resentment in the mainstream gets further fuelled by a sense of being accused and blamed for being one of the better off - this is particularly galling when it seems that it is *they* that are the better off. To use a term like 'institutional racism' is no help in a moment like this; it just further fuels the antipathies, and generates an impasse. 'What institutional racism?' is the outraged cry. 'Just look at the special treatment *they* are getting - they are jumping housing queues and get all sorts of state benefits, whilst we have to wait for years'.

I will take up some additional reasons as to why it is so hard to see what is going on through another anecdote. An organisation convened a workshop to look at and think about the experiences of its black members in order to reflect on its possible unconscious processes. During this workshop one of the participants said: 'I am not responsible for what happened in earlier times and places. I did not colonise Africa and have nothing to do with slavery. I am an individual and I treat others as individuals - some people I like more and others less. I am just like everyone else'.

This is not an uncommon reaction from those in the mainstream; they feel unfairly criticised and accused of doing something, or feel unfairly blamed and made responsible for the sins of their fathers and their fathers. Now, I have a lot of sympathy for what this person is saying. And yet something more complicated must be going on. To understand what that might be we need to recall the fact that racialised discourses conceived the racialised 'us' in two sorts of ways - vertically and horizontally.

By vertically, I mean lineage - the so-called bloodline that is drawn from one's ancestors to the present day. This 'us' stretches back in time, and indeed to the beginnings of time. And by horizontally, I mean typology. This 'us' is an 'us' because all those that belong are of the same 'type' - Caucasian or Black or Mongoloid or whatever. In contrast to the first kind of 'us' that lives in time, the second kind of 'us' spreads across in space.

These versions of 'us' are not usually distinguished, and, depending on the rationalisation one wants to mobilise, one or other of these will be utilised. The participant in the workshop, in saying that, as an individual living in the year 2004, she really is not responsible for the historical processes of colonisation and slavery, is saying that she is not part of a lineage - 'us'. Whilst there might be a bloodline between her and her ancestors, she is saying that she is not responsible for their crimes, and should not be held responsible for the actions that they took. Fair enough.

However, in the here-and-now she is in fact benefiting from privileges accorded to her as a white person by the processes that have become institutionalised. And this occurs *without her having to do anything.* In other words, whilst she is personally not responsible through lineage, she nonetheless benefits by virtue of typology. This occurs because the actions of the ancestors have prepared the world to be biased towards the whites. Thus, whilst this participant's rejection of lineage is understandable and visible, she renders invisible the benefits she derives from typology.

Her cry that she is an individual is an unconscious strategy to avoid acknowledging that she does in fact get benefits from the way that the system is structured. This helps her say, truthfully, 'But I haven't done anything!'. Maybe, but one is never just an individual. One cannot not belong to groups, and the relations between groupings are always power relations. In fact I have been arguing that groupings are generated by power relations. You can see what is happening here. The black is systematically marginalised by virtue of the grouping s/he is part of, whilst the denial of the significance of the groupings by the white person is a means of obscuring the workings of power.

If there is anything at all to the idea of institutional racism, then we would have to admit that those at the centre, those that benefit from the processes of institutionalisation, must have a vested interest in not knowing about the conditions that put them there. This is because any change in the situation would necessarily entail a dilution of the privileges that they are currently accorded.

Disabling politics?

Beyond identity

Tom Shakespeare

Tom Shakespeare argues that the disability movement needs a different approach to identity politics if it is to flourish.

A movement in crisis?

In the 1970s, new organisations such as the Union of Physically Impaired Against Segregation, and the Liberation Network of Disabled People, emerged, and with a radical message: disabled people are an oppressed minority, not unfortunate individuals with medical problems. Thirty years later, research shows that disabled people in the UK remain among the poorest of the poor. Whereas recent political debate has castigated 'sick note Britain', in fact the number of claimants of incapacity benefits is falling, and 30 per cent of disabled people live in poverty. But even this statistic takes no account of the additional costs which disabled people have due to impairment, which are often not met. For example, there is an average £200 unmet weekly gap between income from benefits, and the necessary household expenditure for a disabled person, according to research supported by the Joseph Rowntree Foundation. Moreover, disability does not just cause poverty: it results from it. People in the lowest quintile of income distribution have 2.5 times the annual risk of being impaired than those in the top fifth (www.jrf.org.uk).

The stubbornness and persistence of disabled people's social exclusion suggests that political action by disabled people needs to be correspondingly urgent and vigorous. Yet the UK disability movement in 2005 appears divided and demoralised. The national network of organisations which are controlled by disabled people themselves is the British Council of Disabled People (BCODP). In recent years, it has been riven by internal conflict and external controversy, including a damaging split from the National Council for Independent Living, a project which BCODP had originally initiated. In 2004, the BCODP chief executive, Andy Rickell, was poached by the national disability charity SCOPE. Given that opposition to traditional charities is one of the founding principles of the disability movement, this caused outrage among radical activists. Several of the regional coalitions of disabled people that originally founded the national network recently got together to discuss whether it was time to abandon BCODP, to start again with a more radical and ideologically pure replacement. Meanwhile the Greater London Association of Disabled People, another key organisation within the disability movement, has also been mired in controversy, with staff members being sacked, causing a major dispute between the executive and sections of the membership.

The most visible element of the disability movement, the Disabled People's Direct Action Network (DAN), continues to make headlines with confrontational actions. Yet whereas in the past DAN seemed to reflect the priorities and values of the wider disability community - for example, protesting against inaccessible transport or patronising charity Telethons - it now seems to have lost its way. Increasingly aggressive and uncompromising opposition to the major charities by a hardcore of a few dozen supporters has alienated many ordinary disabled people who used to turn out by the hundreds to support demonstrations. Communiqués from DAN now read like the rantings of an ultra-left groupuscule, rather than a coherent set of achievable political demands. The idea of winning hearts and minds has given way to self-indulgent posturing and oppositionalism.

If the disability movement is in crisis, then, paradoxically, part of the explanation may be located in its success over recent decades. Despite the persistence of poverty and isolation, many disabled people have seen their opportunities transformed. The Disability Discrimination Act, eventually passed by a reluctant Conservative government, has been given teeth under New Labour. Ironically, decades of collective struggle have resulted in a civil rights framework which relies on individuals taking legal action in cases of discrimination. The current Disability Discrimination Bill further extends civil rights protections to new groups, including people diagnosed with HIV and cancer, and to new areas of society; for example it gives local authorities a positive duty to promote equality for disabled people.

London's Disability Capital conference earlier in 2005 showed how much progress had been made: for example, by the end of the financial year 2005-6, all London's buses will be accessible. The Greater London Authority, the Metropolitan Police and many other organisations are working directly with disabled people and taking their issues seriously. Meanwhile, direct payments for disabled people to replace dependency on care with choice and independence are becoming more widely adopted across the UK: there was an 80 per cent increase in uptake between 2002-3 and 2003-4. There is better provision for disabled people, there is more awareness of disability as an equal opportunities issue, and young disabled people now take for granted what their elders fought for throughout the 1970s and 1980s.

One example of the influence of disability rights thinking has been the transformations in some charities. Twenty years ago, slogans such as 'rights not charity' and 'piss on pity' were commonplace on disability demonstrations. There was a clear dividing line between organisations 'of' disabled people and organisations 'for' disabled people. The former were democratic and took a civil rights approach to disabled people, were staffed and controlled by disabled people themselves, and were consequently eligible to join BCODP. The latter were patronising and unaccountable, promoted segregated living and education, and were run by non-disabled professionals and 'the great and the good'. In 2005, it would be hard to find a major disability charity that did not use the language of choices and rights, or which had not at the very least instituted mechanisms for disabled people to be consulted; and often disabled people are in formal control of such organisations. SCOPE, for example, recently announced that it would cease operating segregated residential or educational establishments. Disabled people are in a majority on its ruling Council. The organisation reserves many of its top jobs for disabled people. Launching the 'Time to get equal campaign', SCOPE enlisted Nelson Mandela to support its call for an end to disablism and the promotion of disabled people's rights in every area of society.

In a changed world, where traditional charities could become formally eligible to join the BCODP, it is unclear what being a radical disability activist now means. The persistence of poverty and social exclusion, despite the success of civil rights legislation, leaves the movement in a quandary over what should be done next. Many of the leaders and theorists and activists of the disability movement have either moved into influential jobs in the establishment, or have retired or died. As a consequence, the movement still relies on the slogans and demands that made sense twenty years ago. Activists continue to boycott SCOPE, believing it to be the oppressive organisation which they remember from their childhoods. In the absence of good ideas about future strategies, demonstrators shout the familiar slogans or denounce each other for selling out or going soft, to an ever-smaller audience. The academic field of disability studies is still over-reliant on simplistic and ideological accounts, rather than seeking to generate the powerful insights or useful empirical evidence that could challenge and refresh the political struggle.

For the first time in thirty years, it feels like there is no longer a vibrant disability movement to draw in new generations of disabled people to challenge their oppression and exclusion. But the roots of the current impasse lie in the past.

Origins and contradictions

The disability movement has been called the last liberation movement. Following the civil rights struggles, the women's movement, and the lesbian and gay liberation movement, the grassroots movement of disabled people emerged in Britain and America in the early 1970s.[1] 'Organic intellectuals' like Paul Hunt, Ken and Maggie Davis, Vic Finkelstein, Micheline Mason and many others began meeting to discuss and challenge their status. This was an era where residential institutions were believed to be the best places for disabled people to live. Families and professionals spoke on behalf of disabled people, who were expected to be grateful and thought to be incapable. Having a mental or physical impairment meant that people would be sent to segregated schools; employed in sheltered workshops, if at all; and denied choice or control in their lives. The prevailing cultural assumption was that disability was an

---

1. J. Campbell & M. Oliver, *Disability Politics: understanding our past, changing our future*, Routledge.

individual deficit, caused by an underlying medical problem.

The new breed of disabled activist/intellectual challenged all these ideas. Disability was a form of social oppression, a relationship between people with impairment and a society which discriminated against them. Segregation was part of the problem, not the solution. Charities were patronising and excluding, not benign and noble. Disabled people were the experts on their own lives and demanded to be consulted: their slogan was 'nothing about us, without us'. A political movement was born, and spread rapidly in Britain and in many other countries of the world. 1981 saw the formation both of the BCODP and of Disabled People's International. Ideas such as deinstitutionalisation, independent living, inclusion and civil rights replaced the previous stress on rehabilitation, voluntary action and integration. Disabled people formed their own organisations, and demanded that the mainstream take them seriously as equals. Campaigns for accessible transport shut down town centres. Campaigns against patronising imagery made ITV Telethons unsustainable. This disability direct action did not just achieve instrumental goals: it also issued a symbolic challenge to the traditional idea of disabled people being powerless, incapable and apolitical.

This dual impact - on attitudes to disability, but also on the self-consciousness of disabled people - is highly important. The structural analysis of disability, known in the UK as the social model, relocated the disability problem from the individual to society. In C. Wright Mills's terminology, it made a private problem into a public issue. People were disabled by society, not by their bodies. This conceptual move identified the disabling barriers which needed to be removed in order for disabled people to be included in society. However, it also transformed the self-awareness of disabled people. Rather than being victims of medical tragedy, they were an oppressed group. Rather than feeling sorry for themselves, they could feel a legitimate anger. Disability politics was based on the politics of identity, and the social model proved a potent tool for recruiting new disabled people and making them feel proud and strong.

The disability movement, the disability arts movement, and the developing academic field of disability studies shared a common agenda and were mutually reinforcing. Singer-songwriters such as Johnny Crescendo and the late Ian Stanton provided anthems to make activists feel oppressed, yet powerful. Researchers such as Colin Barnes and Mike Oliver documented discrimination, and theorised the social model and emancipatory research. Over the years, however, a set of stimulating insights from the 1970s became ossified into a disability dogma that has proved difficult to develop or dislodge. Rather than refining the analysis, or responding to changes in the external world, the radical disability community has opted for more of the same. Whereas in other parts of the world - the Nordic countries, the United States, Australia - there have been broader alliances between disabled and non-disabled people, and a more dynamic research agenda, in the UK there has been a separatist and anti-intellectual disability culture, which sometimes appears almost Maoist in its intensity.

Inevitably, this has resulted in problems for the disability movement. Failure to reach out has made strategic alliances with other oppressed groups difficult or impossible. Ideological purity has meant many activists rejecting disability discrimination legislation, because it is not based on a social model definition of disability. Ordinary disabled people do not understand or care about these niceties. They are alienated by a movement which seems inward-looking, sectarian and angry. Participation in disability politics, particularly by younger disabled people, is in decline.

Central to these problems are intrinsic difficulties with the conceptualisation of disability. For example, the social model of disability was largely developed by a group of men with mobility impairments. Extending the analysis to other groups - for example, people with learning difficulties or mental health problems - has proved unstraightforward. Incorporating an awareness

'a set of stimulating insights has become ossified into a disability dogma'

of other oppressions - gender, sexuality and race - has been a slow process. Above all, the social model has led to a denial of the relevance of impairment, either for individuals, or as a political issue. The stress on social barriers and discrimination has produced a corresponding neglect of the personal experience of pain, frailty and weakness. This makes the analysis seem irrelevant to many disabled people who face these difficulties in their everyday lives. Disability is not just a medical issue: impairment is always experienced in a social context. But to reduce disability to social barriers is to create a 'contextual essentialism' which fails adequately to represent the complexity of the phenomenon. The call for disability civil rights law to be based on the social model of disability - the radicals' proposed 'Disabled People's Rights and Freedoms Bill' - would be unworkable, because there would be no protected class specified in the legislation.

The disability movement followed the precedents of other struggles - the labour movement, as well as the identity politics of race, gender and sexuality. While the implicit analogy between disability and other forms of social oppression is challenging and suggestive - particularly to people who have always seen disability as a medical issue - it is also problematic. In the case of women, people from minority ethnic communities, or lesbian and gay people, it is plain that the social problem is caused solely by discrimination and prejudice. Were it not for sexism, racism and homophobia, these groups would be able to live and flourish safely and successfully. Remove the social barriers and treat people equally, and the individuals are liberated. In the case of disability, there is undoubtedly discrimination and prejudice. But even if the barriers are removed, problems still remain. There is an intrinsic difficulty about many impairments which causes difficulty for the individual. Even in the most enlightened and barrier-free society, some disabled people will not be able to do some things, and will be restricted as a result. In other words, in order to flourish, disabled people need different and extra provision. Unlike other oppressions, the challenge of disability is not just to treat people equally and fairly: we are obligated to take additional steps to ensure that needs are met and participation is assured.

This suggests that the disability problem is more profound and more complex even than other areas of equality policy. For example, access to work is important for many groups. Exclusion from work and low pay creates and compounds oppression. Disabled people face discrimination in employment: they are prevented from doing jobs they are qualified for, by inaccessible workplaces and unwelcoming employers. But some disabled people, because of the nature of their impairment, will not be able to do the range of jobs which non-disabled people can do. In some cases, disabled people will not be able to do any form of employment whatsoever. Therefore a just society is required to find ways to support and include and value disabled people outside the system of wage-labour.

This also points to a wider tension. Whereas the culture of the disability movement has always been of the left and the new social movements, some of the agenda has sounded rather neo-liberal. The disability rights critique of the top-down and monolithic nature of the welfare state sat comfortably with a Thatcherite ethos, as did the espousal of values such as independence, freedom and choice. At the heart of disability politics there has been an individualism that opposes collective welfare provision in favour of direct payments to enable individuals to make their own choices. Yet, this liberal rights-based approach has limitations. Many disabled people will not be able to take advantage of the freedom to choose and compete. Not all disabled people want to employ their own staff, or will find it easy to do so. A feminist ethic of interdependence and mutual support may be a more appropriate for many people with learning difficulties or mental health problems, for example. Again, disability challenges us to consider, support and include people who are unable to conform to the standard individual model which has dominated much liberal political philosophy.

By 2006, Government intends to combine the Disability Rights Commission, the Equal Opportunities Commission and the Commission for Racial Equality in a single Commission for Equalities and Human Rights, which will be widened to cover six areas of discrimination: race, gender, sexuality, disability, age and religion. This development highlights the need to deepen our understanding of the differences, as well as the similarities, between disability and other forms of social oppression, and to develop the theoretical underpinnings of disability rights to consider not just how disabled people can be included in the existing structures, but also how the mainstream can be developed and expanded to include people whose abilities, needs and vulnerabilities are very different from the average.

The limits of identity politics?

The clarity and simplicity of disability rights thinking has had benefits. The message is straightforward and appealing to many disabled people. Disability research, unlike other areas of the academy, has remained relevant and engaged and accessible, rather than disappearing into esoteric theory and cultural analysis. However, the movement has atrophied because it looks to the past, not to the future, and because it is built on an identity politics which is self-defeating.

The social movement of disabled people is about the politics of recognition, as well as the politics of redistribution. Disabled people suffer socio-economic injustices, such as marginalisation and deprivation, as well as cultural injustices, such as non-recognition and disrespect. As Nancy Fraser has argued, the intersection of these two forms of politics creates tensions for what she calls 'bivalent collectivities', because the remedies for these oppressions pull in different directions. One response is to treat everyone alike, and to remove arrangements that distinguish and discriminate; the other is to support and valorise group differentiation. The disability movement has always contained these two different impulses: a barriers approach, that seeks to dissolve differences and promote inclusion; and a minority group approach, which seeks a better deal for disabled people and celebrates disabled identity.

Fraser's summary of the new politics could be applied very directly to the disability movement:

> the politics of recognition aims to repair internal self-dislocation by contesting the dominant culture's demeaning picture of the group. It proposes that members of misrecognised groups reject such images in favour of new self-representations of their own making, jettisoning internalised, negative identities and joining collectively to produce a self-affirming culture of their own.[2]

Fraser's analysis of the problems of this approach is also very relevant: the complexity of people's lives is flattened out and the multiplicities and cross-pulls of identity are ignored. At its worst - and at times the disability movement has been guilty of this - such an identity politics becomes repressive, intolerant and conformist. Self-criticism and cultural debate is abandoned. It results in a politics of separatism and enclaves.

Most disabled people share their private and working lives with non-disabled people, and may feel that they have little or nothing in common with other disabled people. They want to overcome and ignore their disability status, not to be locked into it. The ethnic model of disability identity does not work, for them. As Foucault might have said, the problems of speaking politically as

---

2. N. Fraser, 'Rethinking recognition', *New Left Review* 3, 2000, p109.

a disabled person are that one always remains the disabled person who speaks. Disability politics becomes a celebration of victimhood, whereas most disabled people want to be accepted and included as individuals in a society in which neither impairment nor disability is salient.

For Fraser, the alternative to monologism is to treat recognition in terms of the social status of individual members of the group, not as a group specific identity. The goal is for individuals to be treated as equals in interaction with others. Her call for 'non-identitarian politics' relies on 'regulating values that impede parity of recognition of all relevant institutional sites'. Behind the jargon lies the potential of a fresh and different approach to disability politics, which recognises the disrespect and silencing experienced by disabled people, but doesn't rely on valorising an essentialist disability identity and consequently bolstering the boundaries between disabled and non-disabled.

Letting go of old ideologies and the certainty of strong political identities will be painful. But if disability politics is to progress, the movement needs to move on and look outwards. Making alliances with other excluded groups - for example around poverty - could be strategically vital. It will be necessary to recognise that there is a plurality of views in the disability community and that disabled people do not all speak with one voice. Realising that non-disabled people also have a stake in disability - as parents, children, carers, professionals and co-workers - is important. Apart from everything else, many more people become impaired during their lives than are born with impairment: disability is the community which anyone can join.

Disability politics should be about reaching out to more disabled people, and finding more imaginative ways to facilitate their development and quality of life. Resisting the current moves towards charging for services and restricting of access to welfare benefits will be a major priority. A wider, looser, more dynamic and self-critical disability community will not bolster the individual self-identity of disabled people in the same way as the radical politics of old. But the loss will also offer the chance of gaining something much more valuable: true inclusion and recognition as an equal member of wider society.

Racism, cosmopolitanism and contemporary politics of belonging

Nira Yuval-Davis

Nira Yuval-Davis looks at some of the problems of a cosmopolitan politics.

Cosmopolitanism is often constructed as the antithesis of racism, in that it eschews nationalism and/or any other particularistic identity and ideology. However, in my view the picture is considerably more complex than this, and my aim in this article is to explore some aspects of the relationship between cosmopolitanism and questions of belonging and exclusion. In particular, I will argue that a key problem of cosmopolitanism is that, like other universalist approaches, it can be careless about questions of difference and power and ends up operating (consciously or unconsciously) in a racialising and exclusionary top-down manner.

Defining cosmopolitanism

Cosmopolitanism is frequently seen as an alternative to any exclusionary politics of belonging. Ulrich Beck has even argued that that 'to belong or not to belong' is *the* cosmopolitan question. However, this question - and much other writing on cosmopolitanism - implies that belonging is a choice that can always be made, and that one makes it solely for oneself. An alternative question to pose for cosmopolitans would be whether it is capable of including all 'others' (not just selves) as having the choice of belonging. Moreover, a politics based around the idea of belonging as voluntary risks missing key aspects of the systems of social relations that sustain racism, which always involve boundaries that exclude and/or exploit 'the other'. An approach, often from a position of privilege, which simply denies these boundaries or even just their legitimacy, is likely to overlook the processes within which racism and exclusion are able to flourish.

Cosmopolitanism is by its nature a slippery concept, since it tends to reject fixed categories and notions. In the introduction to their book on cosmopolitanism, Sheldon Pollock and co argued that it: 'may be a project whose conceptual content and pragmatic character are not only as yet unspecified but also must always escape positive and definite specification, precisely because specifying cosmopolitanism positively and definitely is an uncosmopolitan thing to do'.[1] Notwithstanding this view, for the purposes of this article it is useful to characterise two broad trends within cosmopolitanism.[2] One approach sees cosmopolitanism as a form of belonging which is detached and fluid, avoiding any fixed notions of boundaries. A representative of this approach is John Urry's 'cultural citizen' (in *Consuming Places*, 1995) - one who operates on the surface, travels frequently and feels at home everywhere and nowhere. The other approach remains based on local attachments, but conceptualises the national as expanding into the international and the transnational. This is where discussions on global citizenship and human rights legislation belong, for example those promoted

---

1. See C.A. Breckenridge, S. Pollock, H.K. Bhabha & D. Chakrabarty (eds), *Cosmopolitanism*, Duke University Press 2002, p1.
2. Following Eleonore Kofman in 'Figures of the Cosmopolitan: privileged nationals and national outsiders', paper presented at the Cosmopolitanism and Europe conference, Royal Holloway, April 2004.

by David Held (in *Democracy and the Global Order*) and Mary Kaldor (in *Global Civil Society: An answer to war*).

Whatever the nature of people's conceptualisation of cosmopolitanism, it is important to remember that discussions on cosmopolitanism will always be closely related to specific cultural and philosophical traditions, and specific constructions of other forms of nationalisms and belonging. Thus the construction of cosmopolitanism in Germany, with its hegemonic history as ethno-nationalism, would be much more hostile to nationalism than, for example, American, or even British contructions, with their hegemonic histories of more civi-nationalisms.[3] Cosmopolitan standpoints are also firmly situated in the social locations of the bearers of the cosmopolitan ideology and their intersected positions in terms of class, ethnicity, gender, etc. Zygmunt Bauman has argued that elites have always been more cosmopolitan than other strata of the population (see, for example, his article in *Soundings* 29); and Nina Werbner has argued that the forced hybridity and cosmopolitanism of migrant labourers in the West is vastly different from the celebrated nomadism and travelling cosmopolitanism of the professional and intellectual classes.[4] Thus, cosmopolitanism is always situated, something that is sometimes unrecognised by its theorists.

It may help to understand the connection between cosmopolitanism, racism and universalism if we look at some of the arguments within anti-racist politics. One fundamental division here can be seen in different visions of a non- or anti-racist society. The universalist vision argues that all people need to be treated the same, especially in the public sphere. For others, the key is a politics of recognition, claiming public acceptance of multiculturalism and affirmative action practices as a precondition for reaching a non-racialised society (see Tariq Modood in *Soundings* 29). The universalists see public acceptance of forms of difference as a practice of racialisation and discrimination - a reification of boundaries. The pluralists accuse the universalists of recognising and legitimising only majoritarian discourse, which is usually

---

3. This notion of situated cosmopolitanism is the focus of the PhD dissertation of my student, Ulrike Vieten, who is comparing German and British discourses on cosmopolitanism.
4. For example, in her 1999 article, 'Global pathways: working class cosmopolitans and the creation of transnational ethnic worlds', *Social Anthropology*, 7:17-35.

western-centric, heterosexist and middle-class in nature; and of rendering invisible the standpoint and interest of excluded minorities. (This position has been argued not only by anti-racists but also by feminists and other identity social movements.)

Before stating my position in relation to these difficult questions, I want to discuss three examples which might shed some light on them: the French legislation against wearing headscarves and other visible signifiers of religion in the public sphere; the contemporary plight of refugees in Europe and elsewhere; and - last but not least - the complex set of issues relating to 'human rights', and what has come to be called 'humanitarian militarism'.

The 'headscarves affair'

The 'headscarves affair' encapsulates some of the key issues involved in an apparently universalist and secularist approach to ethnicity. After several years of stormy public debates and the expulsion of several girls from French schools for wearing Muslim headscarves, on the grounds that they were breaking the requirement of school uniforms, France has recently passed specific legislation which demands the exclusion of any visible forms of religious attachment from French schools and other public institutions. This was done in the name of a neutral and universalist public sphere, and a strict separation between religion and the state. Although the law is couched in general terms, the main controversy has been about Muslims in general and Muslim girls in particular. Banning headscarves has been seen as part of the civilising mission of French republicanism - saving Muslim girls from the barbarian oppressive custom of wearing headscarves. In what has become a familiar pattern, symbolic fights about the character and boundaries of the nation have come to be embodied in the appearance of girls: women's dress (dare I say fashion?) is being invested in as a border battlefield.[5]

It is interesting to note at this point the effect of this law on Jewish boys, who are no longer allowed to wear 'kippas' on their heads at state schools. In a recent interview, a French Rabbi pointed out that most religious Jewish boys in France attend Jewish religious schools these days, so that this law will not have a major effect on the Jewish community. In other words, the prohibition

---

5. For the detailed argument see my book *Gender and Nation*, Sage 1997.

against the wearing of visible signifiers of religious attachment is not really valid in all parts of the public sphere. They are allowed - or actually required - to be worn in schools and other institutions which are under the control of religious community leaders. This means that, far from 'these poor Muslim girls' being saved from the clutches of the Mullahs, from now on, if they want to wear Muslim headgear in schools, they will have to attend schools over which these religious leaders have total control. Many contemporary Muslim girls want to wear headscarves not to signify their religious submission, but as a defiant signifier of minority identity, as part of an anti-racist mode. Such girls are likely to find their plight now made much more difficult, inasmuch as they are frequently involved in a dual fight against sexist community leaders as well as racist majoritarian society. Closing down majoritarian public spaces to this form of minority identity display has the effect of closing off yet another option for young Muslim women.

Thus the French public sphere has not become more universalist as a result of this law; it has become more homogeneously western-centric. It is ensuring that it remains 'unpolluted' by public signifiers of difference. Any form of cosmopolitanism that endorsed such a variant of 'universalism' would thereby incorporate into itself a racialised and exclusionary discourse - in the name of supposed 'neutrality'.

Refugees and other 'people on the move'

For writers such as Hannah Arendt, and more recently Giorgio Agamben, the refugee has come to symbolise 'the other', who is displaced, has no rights and whose life is in danger. The way refugees are treated is thus indicative of a system's approach to inclusivity and belonging. There are some who argue that cosmopolitanism, in the form of world government, offers answers to questions of international human rights and the protection of refugees and other displaced people. In this section I consider some aspects of this issue.

Although the term refugees was first applied to those who escaped the French regime in the eighteenth century, it was not until the establishment of the League of Nations after the first world war that the first international organisation to deal with refugees was established (the Inter-Governmental Committee on Refugees). After the second world war UNHCR (the United Nations High Commission on Refugees) was established and the UN

Convention on Refugees was passed. Since the establishment of this machinery the 'business' of refugees has grown enormously. The number of countries in which the UNHCR operates grew from 16 in 1962 to 123 in 1996. Furthermore there are many millions of internally displaced people in the world who are not classified as refugees (some estimates put the figure at 20-22 million); there is also an estimated worldwide total of 33 million illegal immigrants. The UN Population Division reported in October 2002 that it estimated that in 2000 there were about 175 million people in total living in countries which were not their country of birth - double the amount in 1975 (and this estimate, of course, excludes illegal migrants).

Alongside this large increase in the numbers of people in migration, there has been a radical change in attitudes and policies towards refugees and asylum seekers (the term asylum seeker applies to people who are not formally recognised as refugees, but who are currently actively seeking to be recognised as such by particular states). These changes have come about largely as a result of the end of the cold war and the growth of the securitisation agenda, especially after the events of 11 September 2001 in the USA. In the new situation, the old postwar concept of universal rights for refugees and other migrants has more or less vanished. In the newly globalised world, 'rights' tend to be restricted to those who have skills to offer to countries of immigration. (This is in marked contrast to a western rhetoric of human rights that addresses itself to the nature of whole regimes, something I will look at in the next section.) The rest can be disregarded - they are seen as what Zygmunt Bauman has called surplus to requirements, as human waste. In a similar vein Giorgio Agamben has described refugees as living in a state of 'bare life'.[7]

In a development from Hannah Arendt's work, Agamben argues that in the nation-state system, the 'sacred and inalienable rights of man' turn out to be called into question at the very point at which they are claimed by those who are no longer citizens of a state. Agamben's reflections on modern 'bare life' are of crucial importance; many - maybe even most - contemporary asylum seekers exist in a state that is usefully characterised in this way. However, my argument

---

6. See his essay in *Mediactive: Asylum* (issue 4 spring 2005), 'Who is seeking asylum, and from what?'.
7. Giorgio Agamben, 'We Refugees', www.egs.edu/faculty/agamben/agamben-we-refugees.html, p1.

is that they are in this position not because they are refugees, but precisely because they are *not* legally recognised as refugees. The increasing numbers of those who remain as asylum *seekers*, rather than actually attaining the status of refugees, show the gap between the legal framework and the reality of people's lives. In the postwar era refugees that have been recognised as such have generally acquired some rights and protection in international law: although such law tends to be 'toothless' in comparison with national state laws, it is complied with, at least formally, by all states. The problem is that, while ostensibly complying with the rights and regulations of international law concerning refugees, most states these days have created a situation in which it is more and more difficult - if not virtually impossible - to acquire that legal status. More and more people who some years ago would have been entitled to the rights and protection of the status of a refugee today have no legal means to obtain it, and are pushed into other, unprotected, forms of migration. It is really these 'people on the move' (as the UN describes them) - unprotected and 'undocumented' migrants, unable to attain the status of refugees, and constructed outside any national or international law - who exist in a state of 'bare life'. Thus international law could in theory maintain the human rights of those who have lost their citizenship rights in their home country, but it fails to do so.

> 'the old postwar concept of universal rights for refugees has vanished ... rights tend to be restricted to those who have skills to offer'

It is also worthy of note that recently there have been many attempts to undermine the legal status and rights of refugees, even for the few who have managed to attain this position. For example, it has been argued that the status of refugee should no longer be a permanent status; it should be liable to be removed at any point at which it can be decided that 'the homeland' has become 'safe'. This would mean that, though they were not living in the conditions of 'bare life', such as are experienced by undocumented migrants, refugees would be compelled to live the life of the permanently insecure, unable to plan futures for themselves and their families. Thus the postwar international institutions have not provided the protection that they proclaimed in their first flush of youth.

There are millions of people for whom global protective legislation does not guarantee non-exclusion; nor does it protect them from racialisation and persecution. This means that a cosmopolitan proposal for the construction of world government (such as put forward by David Held, for example) offers no real social and political alternative to racialised exploitation and exclusion at the global level. The evidence seems to indicate that international frameworks are only as strong as the ideological and material contexts within which they exist.

'Human rights' and 'humanitarian militarism'

For many years, and particularly since the end of the cold war, support for human rights has been a rallying cry for people all over the world, not as citizens of specific states, but as part of the human race. As such, support for human rights on a global scale could be seen as cosmopolitan par excellence.

Major steps for the human rights mobilisation have included the 1994 UN Conference on Human Rights in Vienna, and, more recently, the establishment of the International Criminal Court - something for which feminist and other human rights international activists have been fighting for a long time.

However, there are a number of problems with the human rights agenda. Costas Douzinas, Head of the Human Rights Centre at Birkbeck College, London, argues that recent developments have actually seen the end of human rights, because they have become defined in over-legalistic terms, and have lost their utopian aspect. As such: 'while they remain an instrument of reform and, occasionally, a sophisticated tool for analysis … they stop being the tribunal of history'.[8]

Meanwhile, Michael Ignatieff, Head of the Centre for Human Rights at Harvard University, sees human rights as threatened for almost the opposite reasons. For him the proliferation of declarations and treaties is seen as dangerous not because human rights have been losing their utopian appeal, but because they have been losing their pragmatic appeal. Ignatieff warns against 'elevating the moral and metaphysical claims made on behalf of human rights'.[9] For him, 'human rights' is a specific form of politics with a minimalist kernel, aimed at defending people's rights to free agency, the ability to make decisions and to be protected from abuse and oppression. Thus the Ignatieff argument is based on a

---

8. Costas Douzinas, *The end of human rights*, Hart 2000, p380.
9. Michael Ignatieff, *Human Rights as Politics and Idolatry*, Princeton University Press 2001, p53.

quite limited view of human rights, which exists within a specified legal framework, while Douzinas has an ethical and mobilising conception of justice.

Ignatieff's conception of human rights is based on negative freedoms (to use Isaiah Berlin's term); and this is too minimalist even for Amy Gutman, the Princeton professor who provided the introduction to Ignatieff's book. Thus she points out (p ix) that 'the right to subsistence is as necessary for human agency as a right against torture … Starving people have no more agency than people subject to cruel and unusual punishment'. This contrast between a negative (free from) and positive (free to) approach to human rights is one that is widely debated both within the networks of human rights activists, and between such activists and those who are critical of the concept of human rights. Such differences and difficulties are reflected within the UN institutions. While the original Universal Declaration of Human Rights adopted by the UN in 1948 did indeed encompass civil, political, economic, social and cultural rights, these spheres were separated out in subsequent covenants, under the influence of the cold war. Civil and political rights (largely negative, 'freedom from', rights) were given primacy in global human rights, while economic, social and cultural rights (positive, 'freedom to', rights) received much less attention. This emphasis was particularly strongly supported by the US.

Needless to say, this does not mean that the fall of the Soviet Union and the end of the cold war has altered the approach of the US. In fact the selective and minimalist approach to human rights, and the notion that they encompass only civil and political rights, coincides precisely with the neo-liberal agenda, which has been strengthened by the collapse of alternative systems.

Alongside this development, the other major controversial issue in international human rights related policies has been the assertion of the right - or even the duty - of the UN, or of some states, to intervene forcefully in the affairs of other states, those in which human rights violations have taken place. A major argument against such interventions is that the basis of international relations, as well as of the UN, has been constructed as inter-national, not trans-national; there is thus no space for intervening in what are considered to be the internal affairs of other states. Such interventions are likely to threaten the stability of international state order. On the other hand, one can argue that the impetus behind the establishment of the UN, and especially for the

1951 Universal Declaration of Human Rights, was to provide an institutional framework capable of ensuring that the atrocities of the Nazi regime should never again be allowed to happen. The failure of the international community to intervene in Rwanda in time to prevent the major genocide there has been seen by many as something that must be avoided in future. And indeed one effect of the end of the cold war has been an increase in the ability of some states, or the UN, to make international military interventions, without thereby posing a major threat to international stability.

In the post-cold-war era there has arisen a new phenomenon - 'humanitarian militarism'; this describes an approach which advocates military intervention (thus far western-led) in specific states, on the grounds of massive abuses of human rights within such states, whether these result from the nature of the regime itself or from the militarised conflicts taking place within them. Such interventions - especially those sanctioned by the UN - have been seen by many as an inevitable step in an effort to transform the globe into a place where everyone can be protected through support of their human rights. There is a clear normative basis for this 'humanitarian militarism': not only that universal human rights have a higher normative value than state sovereignty, but also that there is a complementary need to fight against terrorism. 'Terrorism' is seen as being promoted by rogue states, or as permitted by other 'failing states' that are too weak to deal with terrorist groups operating within their territories; outside intervention is thus needed in such states in order to maintain local and global security. Although already hailed by the Reagan government as the core of its foreign policy, the fight against terrorism has become the inseparable twin of 'human rights abuses' as a rhetorical device for the justification of international intervention, especially since the September 2001 events.

Critics of this approach (such as David Chandler) argue that, although 'human rights' discourse talks about human empowerment and recognition, in reality it offers less to people than was formerly provided by more positive forms of international aid. As the emphasis has shifted away from assistance in providing for people's material wants, the withdrawal of such assistance has actually been used as a weapon in the battle against terrorism.[10] Thus UN

---

10. David Chandler, *From Kosovo to Kabul: Human Rights and International Intervention*, Pluto Press 2002.

World Food Programme aid was withdrawn from Afghanistan after the
September 2001 bombings in the United States; relief was suspended from
Sierra Leone after the military coup; and in the aftermath of 'humanitarian
interventions' in Kosovo and Iraq people have had less access to food aid than
before the interventions. In the case of Afghanistan, although some women in
Kabul have been able to take off the chador (many prefer not to) and - more
importantly - to go to school and work, in most of the rest of the country little
if anything has changed in this respect; the main difference is that the gangs
that control the growth of opium, which was banned under the Taliban, now
have more power than ever.

It is an open question as to whether or not such deployment of 'human
rights' discourse in fact serves to delegitimise the concept altogether.[11] What
is clear, however, is that, in spite of their foundational universalistic inclusive
nature, 'human rights', like other cosmopolitan constructions, can be - and
are being - used in a variety of racialised ways, as well as being used in struggles
to resist them.

Concluding discussion

Some critics have claimed that there is an inherent flaw in human rights
discourse, in that it is unable to establish clear foundations for the substance
and character of some of the new positive rights its proponents have proclaimed.
The argument is that if the discourse of rights tries to embrace more than a
neutral protection of means, and to include within its framework ethical and
value-laden ends, or if it bases its claims on any external authority, this tends
to undercut the universality and democratic content of rights (*From Kosovo to
Kabul*, p119). Chandler's view is that arguments about the substance or content
of human rights, or the means of implementing and guaranteeing them, cannot
be resolved through democratically accountable mechanisms, because the very
nature of such debate, in invoking the concept of rights, serves to repose
political questions of power and distribution as moral absolutes, which then
become subject to external or legal interpretation through international

11. For a development of this argument see Nira Yuval-Davis, 'Human rights, human
security and contemporary gendered politics of belonging', in L. Basch, P. Clough & K.
Timothy (eds.), *Facing Global Capital, Finding Human Security: a Gendered Critique*,
Feminist Press, forthcoming.

institutions or domestic and international courts.

In other words, like Douzinas, Chandler links 'the end of human rights' to the growing power of judicial authorities in this field. Unlike Douzinas, however, he sees this development as part of the growing hegemony of a normative discourse, rather than the end of it. He also differs from Ignatieff, however, in that he sees the spread of human rights politics as disabling rather than facilitating human agency.

Crucially - and unlike much contemporary discourse - Chandler sees popular grassroots democracy as the progressive alternative to top-down human rights discourse: it is more usual for rights-based approaches to see such grassroots democracy as an automatic expression of human rights. This is an important counter-argument. However, I cannot fully share Chandler's trust in 'the people'. We all know that Hitler (and Bush - not that I equate the two) was supported by a majority of the electorate. And we all know that anti-asylum-seeker and other racist agendas are driven everywhere by the view that they are good 'vote catchers'; we also know that minority rights - including cultural rights - often need to be protected by top-down legislation, in order to counter racist practices in housing, work and other public arenas.

So what is the solution to these dilemmas - if any - and how, if at all, does it relate to cosmopolitanism?

In her recent *Soundings* article on cosmopolitanism (issue 24), Chantal Mouffe recommends a multipolar world order as the only answer to the tyranny of the contemporary unipolar world, which takes for granted western culture and norms as the highest form of achievement, and shows no sensitivity to different cultural traditions. She argues that, in order to create channels for the legitimate expression of dissent, we need to envisage a pluralistic world order, 'constructed around a certain number of great spaces and genuine cultural poles'. Although I can see merits in Mouffe's proposal, I can also see in it great problems. Her discourse in this article does not distinguish between social and spatial locations, or between cultural identities and political value systems. She therefore runs the risk that her proposed solution could be seen as reproducing the essentialised constructions of Huntington's 'clash of civilizations' thesis. She is right to argue that global politics cannot be assumed to be a politics of consensus, as most cosmopolitanism literature does, but her solution offers an insufficiently differentiated notion of a possible agonistic alternative. It is important that dissent within global politics is understood as a question of power. Any hope for emancipatory, inclusive and non-racist polities must be based on a politics of political alliances - rather than on cultural, religious, or racial allegiances.

One solution to the problem posed by the limitations of emancipatory politics when expressed through the appeal to universal human values is offered by Dipesh Chakrabarty. He points out that the universal can only exist as a placeholder; its place is always ultimately usurped by a historical particular seeking to present itself as the universal.[12] In this light, the aim of emancipatory and anti-racist politics could be to aspire to establish a universal which would be as inclusive as possible, at the same time knowing that this is a process and not a goal; perhaps it is in this sense that 'specifying cosmopolitanism positively and definitely' is an uncosmopolitan thing to do.

We cannot - and should not attempt to - construct a homogeneous, or even unified, political order. Rather, we should engage in a transversal dialogue (see *Soundings* 12, special issue on transversal politics, especially my definition there of 'what is transversal politics'), bounded by common political values, informed by recognitions of our differential locations and identifications, and led by a global discourse in which translation, rather than a unitary language, is seen as the cosmopolitan tool.

This article is based on a lecture given to the anti-racist think-tank Agora in Stockholm, February 2005.

---

12. Dipesh Chakrabarty, 'Universalism and Belonging in the Logic of Capital', in *Cosmopolitanism* (for full reference see note 1).

Zionism and the spirit of nations

Jacqueline Rose

Jacqueline Rose *traces genealogies of dissenting
Zionist voices.*

Conceived in the last quarter of the nineteenth century, political Zionism
and psychoanalysis each produced their founding texts in the first decades
of the twentieth; they are companions of the spirit, their journey coterminous,
even if radically divergent as to their ends. Precisely because Zionism had to
make itself out of nothing - create a unity, a language, a homeland where
there was none before - it knows itself as a child of the psyche, a dream, a
figment of the brain. Theodor Herzl, founder of political Zionism and
convener of the first Zionist Congress in 1897, was after all a playwright
before anything else (the first, and until Vaclev Havel, the only political figure
known to have such a beginning). The unconscious, wrote Freud in one of
his most famous definitions, is '*ein andere Schauplatz*', another scene.[1] Herzl's
projects for the creation of a Jewish state all crumbled on their own
diplomatically fuelled grandeur, but he may also, in his magisterial failure,
have been wise to something. Like the unconscious, Zionism had to be staged
(as only a playwright might understand). Zionism was a conjuring act. 'They
escaped to Palestine', Hannah Arendt wrote of the early Zionists, 'as one
might wish to escape to the moon'. Zionism always involved a form of
'insubordination' against reality and the demands of reason. 'The politics of
peoples', declared Arthur Ruppin in 1936, resigning from the organisation
Brit Shalom, which struggled to preserve relations with the Arabs, 'are not

---

1. Sigmund Freud, *The Interpretation of Dreams*, 1900, Standard Edition, 4, p48.

determined by rational considerations but by their instinctive drives'.[2]

As if to say, he who enters here plumbs the depths of the political mind. This makes Zionism, for better and worse, the most wonderful exemplar of the work of the psyche in the constitution of the modern nation-state. Ruppin continues: 'All the economic advantages and rational considerations will not lead the Arabs to relinquish sovereignty over Palestine in favour of the Jews, since, in their eyes, it belongs to them.' Reason will not settle it. You cannot have an argument with a dream. 'Men are ruled by the simple and the fantastic', Herzl states in conversation with the Bavarian nobleman, Baron Maurice de Hirsch. 'It is astonishing [...] with what little intelligence the world is ruled.'[3] 'Believe me', he continues to Hirsch in a subsequent letter, 'the politics of an entire people - especially one that is scattered all over the world - can only be made out of *imponderables that float high in the thin air* (cited *Herzl*, p137).

*

If Zionism knows its own unconscious dimension, there are, however, two very different ways in which such an acknowledgement can take shape. Herzl's way is the most obvious: '"A flag? What's that? A stick with a cloth rag?" No, a flag, sir, is more than that [...] It is indeed the only thing for which [men] are willing to die in masses, provided one educates them for it' (cited *Herzl*, p143). But there is another strand to Zionism, to be found in writers like Martin Buber, Hannah Arendt, Hans Kohn and Ahad Ha'am, which provides the profoundest analysis of these dangers, dangers which - it is my argument in this essay - have to be understood as much in psychic as political terms. These dissenters were articulate and vocal throughout the crucial period leading up to the formation of the nation, although inside Israel their voices have been mostly silenced since. Hannah Arendt's ideas, writes Amnon Raz-Krakotzkin, 'became irrelevant when what she foresaw came to be real'; they were deemed 'unrealistic' in proportion as 'reality' proved her correct.[4] It is for me therefore

2. Cited Georges Bensoussan, *Une Histoire intellectuelle et politique du sionisme*, Fayard 2002, p474.
3. Herzl, conversation with Maurice de Hirsch, 2 June 1895, *Complete Diaries* Vol 1, cited in Amos Elon, *Herzl*, Holt, Rhinehart and Winston 1975, p136.
4. Amnon Raz-Krakotzkin, 'Binationalism and Jewish Identity: Hannah Arendt and the Question of Palestine', in Stephen E. Aschheim (ed), *Hannah Arendt in Jerusalem*, University of California Press 2001, p169.

one of the strengths of Zionism - one of the reasons why it should not be dismissed, even or especially by its critics - that it could have produced this dissenting analysis from within. All these writers witnessed in their lifetime the triumph of the Jewish nation that none of them could have confidently predicted, but the shape it assumed before their eyes made this less a cause for elation than for lament. This did not stop them from espousing the Jewish cause nor indeed from advocating a Jewish home in Palestine. But they each believed that Zionism could have taken a different path from the one it proclaimed - and still proclaims - as its destiny. All of them except Arendt took up residence in Palestine. Imagine how hard it must have been to pull against the drift, to have been anything other than euphoric in 1948. Today theirs is the still resonant, melancholic, counter-narrative to the birth of a nation-state.

At the heart of Zionism, writes Martin Buber in his article, 'Zionism and "Zionism"', published on 27 May 1948, two weeks after the establishment of Israel, there is an 'internal contradiction that reaches to the depths of human existence'.[5] There are two notions of national rebirth. Both require a return to Palestine. But whereas one desires to become a 'normal' nation, with 'a land, a language and independence', the other, outside political time, aims to restore the spirit: 'the spirit would build the life, like a dwelling, or like flesh' (p221). These two tendencies, which have been 'running about next to each other from ancient times', represent the division between the task of truth and justice, and the wish - 'all too natural' - to be like other nations (p221). Like Arendt, Buber takes Zionism to task for being the real form of assimilation. 'The Zionists were the only ones who sincerely wanted assimilation', writes Arendt, 'namely, "normalisation" of the people ("to be a people like all other peoples")'.[6] 'Of all the many kinds of assimilation in the course of our history', Buber had written in 1939, 'this nationalist assimilation is the most terrifying, the most dangerous'.[7] The ancient Hebrews did not succeed in becoming a normal nation: 'Today,' he writes in 1948, 'the Jews are

5. Reprinted in Paul Mendes-Flohr (ed), *A Land of Two Peoples - Martin Buber on Jews and Arabs*, Oxford University Press 1983, p220.
6. In 'Zionism Reconsidered', 1944, in *The Jew as Pariah*, p146.
7. Martin Buber, 'The Spirit of Israel and the World of Today' [1939], reprinted in Nahum N. Glatzer (ed), *On Judaism*, Schocken 1967, p185.

succeeding at it to a terrifying degree' ('Zionism and "Zionism"', p221). Zionism should not have created, or tried to create, a normal nation.

Buber's distinction between the spirit building the life and the normality of nations is therefore mapped onto a distinction between truth and justice, and terror or fear: 'today the Jews are succeeding to a terrifying degree' (that a nation's triumph, as much as external threat, can be a cause for fear is not something we hear in Israel today). 'Where,' he asks, 'do truth and justice determine our deeds?' ('Zionism and "Zionism"'p221). Most simply, crucially, Buber is objecting to the injustice being perpetrated against the Arabs: 'what nation will allow itself to be demoted from the position of majority to that of minority without a fight?' (p223). But Buber's argument contains a complex psychic dimension. His question: 'Where do truth and justice determine our deeds?' in fact continues 'either inwardly or outwardly?' He then adds in parenthesis, 'I said "inwardly" because unruliness directed outwards inevitably brings on unruliness directed inwards' (p221). Buber is warning that the outward injustice towards the Arabs does not only harm them, but will also have damaging consequences inside the new nation. Far from securing its future and safety, it will threaten its inner cohesion, bringing havoc, or 'unruliness', in its train. Not only will the nation be the object of attack ('what nation will allow itself to be demoted without a fight'), but its inner life, *by the mere fact of becoming a normal nation*, will corrupt itself, will not survive.

Almost before the first shot was fired in 1948, Buber is suggesting both that Israel will be the object of aggression *and* that it will fail in its attempt to locate the aggressor purely on the outside. There is a crucial lesson here - criticising Israel does not involve denying that she has enemies. Violence will come home to roost. In psychoanalytic parlance, the nation will fail to project. Seeing the enemy as outside threat only, Israel was sowing the seeds of long term damage within. 'Everything that did stay to challenge Israel', writes Edward Said in his essay 'Zionism from the Standpoint of its Victims', 'was viewed not as something *there*, but as something *outside* Israel and Zionism bent on its destruction - from the outside'.[8] One effect of course has been to render virtually invisible, or non-existent as equal citizens, the Arab Israelis

---

8.   Edward Said, 'Zionism from the Standpoint of Its Victims', *The Question of Palestine*, p89.

inside the nation. In September 2003, the Or Commission Report recommended: 'The State of Israel has an interest in acting to erase the stain of discrimination against the Arab citizens'.[9]

This is not, it should be stressed, the kind of criticism that bemoans the nation's subsequent betrayal of itself (a betrayal represented for many by the occupation of 1967). It is a far more radical critique. For Buber, the soul of the nation was forfeit from the day of its creation: 'We have full independence, a state and all that appertains to it', Buber writes even more urgently in the following year. 'But where is the nation in the state? And where is that nation's spirit?' (*Land of Two Peoples*, p250). Which is not to say, it might need stressing, that Israel should cease to exist, but that the nation will perhaps only survive if it takes the fullest measure of this founding dilemma. Today, David Grossman makes the same link as Buber between inward and outer havoc, between blindness and injustice. He makes a similar plea. The average Israeli, he writes in his despatches from Jerusalem, refuses introspection, dreading the 'disconcerting and menacing emotions it might provoke': 'He dreads that they will kindle disquieting questions about the justice of his actions.'[10]

If Zionism taps the unconscious, then it seems to me that what Buber is almost saying is that *it should stay there*. An intangible dimension, spiritual and ethical, should give to this new collective being its shape. Again, this ethical dimension has nothing to do with Ben-Gurion trumpeting the unique moral mission of Israel (which leads in its worst forms to the insistence voiced repeatedly by a number of those I interviewed in 2002, such as Zalman Shoval, former Israeli Ambassador to the United States, that America supports Israel because as nations they share a unique moral character).

As I see it, Buber is lifting into the realm of politics the complex relations that hold between unconscious and conscious life. Freud had a formula for the aims of analysis - '*Wo es war soll ich werden*' - where it was, so shall I come to be. In the time of Strachey's notorious translation, 'Where Id was there Ego shall be', English speakers understood this as the need to replace the unconscious with the all-knowing ego; Lacan's counter-translation - 'There

---

9. 'What Needs to Be Done', announcement of opening of Conference of the Sikkuy 'Or Commission Watch' Project, *Ha'aretz*, 18 June 2004.
10. David Grossman, 'Death as a Way of Life', May 2001, *Death as a Way of Life*, p115.

where it was so should, must I come to be' proposes that the I should cede before the unpredictable movements of the unconscious. Buber quite explicitly makes the link between the I and the nation: 'The typical individual of our times,' he wrote in his 1939 lecture 'The Spirit of Israel and the World of Today', 'holds fast to *his expanded ego, his nation*' (p180). Similarly Hans Kohn will argue that Zionism, which should have offered a new model of nationhood, has fallen prey to the '*naïve and self-limited egoism* of sacred faith'.[11] The nation should not be normal. Instead of owning others or itself, instead of battening down, fixing itself, knowing and owning too much, let it slip between analogies: the spirit, Buber writes, should build the life 'like a dwelling or like flesh'.

What would a nation look like constituted on some such terms? If this is messianism, it is a far cry from the messianism on which the nation has predominantly fashioned itself. Utopian but resolutely anti-apocalyptic, Buber's Zionism was not political Zionism, but Zionism devoted to the life of the spirit and, drawing on the Hasidic tradition, to the sanctification of everyday life. 'The grand Eastern Jewish creation of Hasidim', writes Arnold Zweig in 1920, 'pours into the most prosaic of daily activities, into the most immediate call of the day'.[12] Much follows from this. Such a Zionism does not require the ever-increasing ingathering of the exiles: 'We need for this land as many Jews as it is possible economically to absorb, but not in order to establish a majority against a minority' (Buber, *Land of two peoples*, p183). Nor the denial of the Arabs' political rights: 'Jewish immigration must not cause the political status of the present inhabitants to deteriorate' (p183); nor the conquering of the land: 'we are not obliged to conquer the land, for no danger is in store for our spiritual essence or our way of life from the population of the land' (p222).

Concretely, what Buber proposed was not partition, which he saw as a 'slicing' or breaking apart of the land, but a 'covenant' of two independent nations with equal political rights, 'united in the enterprise of developing their common homeland and in the federal management of shared matters' (p222). The only thing to be sanctified for Buber is 'work in common', by which he

11. Hans Kohn, 'Nationalism', 1921-22, *The Jew - Essays from Buber's Journal Der Jude*, edited Arthur A. Cohen, University of Alabama Press 1980, p27.
12. Arnold Zweig, *The Face of East European Jewry*, University of California Press 2004, p11.

means in common with the Arabs - not the land, not the state (there should not be a sovereign state), only the slow pacings of daily tasks. For Buber, writing in 1948, the fact that Zionism failed in this task, made itself sovereign so as to enter into the world of nations, is nothing short of a political and spiritual catastrophe: 'This sort of "Zionism" blasphemes the name of Zion' (p221).

Compare ChaimWeizmann, inter-war president of theWorld Zionist Organisation and first president of Israel, in whose discourse the plea for normality is thunderous: 'the greatest challenge to the creative forces of the Jewish people, its redemption from the *abnormalities* of exile'; 'scattered among foreign cultures […] our life displays something *abnormal*'; 'a decisive step towards *normality* and true emancipation'; 'our relations to the other races and nations would become more *normal*'; 'We shall revert to *normal* […] "like unto all the nations"'.[13] For Buber, on the contrary, the nation becomes normal - in this he is very close to psychoanalysis - at the cost of perverting itself.

*

Hans Kohn, one of Buber's closest disciples and friends, had been a devoted Zionist since 1909 when he had joined the Bar Kochba students organisation in Prague; he had arrived in Palestine in 1923. Explaining his decision to resign from the Zionist Organisation after the Arab riots of 1929, he writes: 'We pretend to be innocent victims. Of course the Arabs attacked us in August. Since they have no armies, they could not obey the rules of war'.[14] 'We are obliged', he insists, 'to look into the deeper causes of this revolt', such as the fact that we have not 'even once made a serious attempt at seeking through negotiations the consent of the indigenous peoples' (p99) (compare Sharon, refusing even the possibility of a negotiated settlement and unilaterally withdrawing from Gaza today).

Writing of the suppression of the Arab revolt, Kohn then warns against a falsely triumphant 'victorious peace': 'Just like the powers in the [First] World

13. Weizmann, *Trial and Error*, p 418; 'On World Citizenship and Nationalism', Prague, 27 March 1912, *Letters and Papers*, Volume 1, Series B, pp89, 91; 'The Jewish People and Palestine', 1936 statement before the Palestine Royal Commission, p12; 'States are not Given', Address at UPA Campaign Banquet, London, 28 January 1948, *Letters and Papers*, Series B, 1, p 687.
14. In 'Zionism is not Judaism', *A Land of Two Peoples* (see note 5), p98.

War, we have declared that we would gladly make peace if only we were strong enough' (p99). Such strength, he suggests, is illusory. It will have to feed on itself. Politics in this guise is both superficial (fails to look into the 'deeper cause' of this revolt), and endless. Interminable, violence will inscribe itself into the heart of the nation: 'I believe that it will be possible to hold Palestine and continue to grow for a long time. This will be done first with British aid and then later with the help of our own bayonets - shamefully called *Haganah* [i.e. defensive] - clearly because we have no faith in our own policy. But by that time we will not be able to do without the bayonets' (p99). Looking back in the 1960s, Kohn explains, in an essay called 'Zionism', that it was from A.D. Gordon, an early Zionist and inspiration for many Labour Zionists, that he drew his critique of the militarism of what was to become the Israeli state: 'A people cannot be "redeemed", Gordon taught, by political success, even less by military victory, but only by the spiritual and moral rebirth of the individual.'[15] Kohn has predicted that a nation investing itself in military power will be unable to restrain itself.

Like Buber, from whom he takes his inspiration, Kohn wants *another* type of nationalism, one that reaches, in his words, 'for the stars', neither 'deadly drug' nor 'hypocritical camouflage' for state needs and collective power; it will be 'more loving', 'more attached to the life of the individual' ('the most private and hidden essence of mankind') ('Nationalism', p30). Kohn arrives at his vision after the dark night of the First World War, which he saw as the 'witch's orgy' of the nation state ('Nationalism', Editor's note, p20). He therefore invested in Zionism a belief in a new form of nationhood that would make national war 'as impossible as the religious fanaticism of Saint Bartholomew's Night' (p26). For Kohn, nations were lifting from religious creeds the dangers of territorial expansion and authoritarian violence. In an ideal future, nations must therefore shed the aura of the sacred: 'The sacred rights of the nation [...] will be as incomprehensible as the military and murderous fury released by a disputed interpretation of a Biblical word or form of the sign of the cross' (p26).

Kohn was wrong in his hopes of what was to come, but it is one of the

---

15. Hans Kohn, 'Zionism', in *Living in a World Revolution - My Encounters with History*, Trident 1964, p48.

ironic strengths of his analysis that all its central terms - sacred, violent fury, militarism, religious fanatacism - should return to the heart of Israel's future struggle, both with its neighbours and with itself. At a round table meeting of Israelis and European Jews, organised by the Jewish organization Hanadiv, held in Canisy, Northern France in January 2003, leading *Ha'aretz* journalist Daniel Ben-Simon observed that before the outbreak of the second *intifada* a crucial discussion was taking place inside Israel about the relationship between a secular and religious future for the country - or as he put it, between democracy and clerical fascism. Now it has simply stopped (Arabic has also been taken off the school curriculum).

If Kohn's vision is, as for Buber, also a form of messianism that 'redeems the world', it is also - again like that of Buber - resolutely anti-apocalyptic, seeing its destiny not in the apotheosis, but in a sacrifice, of self (p28). But Kohn goes even further than Buber in plumbing the psychic dimension - the compelling and dangerous force - of nationalism in its modern guise. This passage, worth quoting in full, could almost have been lifted out of Freud's *The Future of an Illusion*:

> The enormous suffering of existence, the enigma of life staring at us eternally, the plethora of all things and connections assaulting us with a destructive gesticulation, the dark beast that inexplicably threatens, keeps arising within us - all these things would be unendurable if a faith, a sustaining world principle, did not bind them into unity and give them meaning and purpose, making the remote and the unsure more familiar through the threads of myth (p26).

Nationalism, the wrong kind, the kind which has become 'absolute', 'an idol', allows you the illusion of mastering the unmasterable: the enigma of life, destructive gesticulations, the dark beast (for Freud, the terrors of nature, the cruelty of Fate, the sufferings imposed by civilisation).[16] It allows you, like the ego, to believe you could be sufficient unto yourself. Similarly, Judah Leon Magnes, first President of the Hebrew University of Jerusalem, another dissenting voice, warned in 1930 in an article interrogatively entitled 'Like All

---

16. *The Future of an Illusion*, 1927, Standard Edition, 21, p18.

the Nations?': 'There is the *Wille zur Macht*, the state, the army, the frontiers […] now we are to be masters in our own home.'[17]

'Must not,' Freud asks, ' the assumptions that determine our political regulations be called illusions as well?' (*Future of an Illusion*, p34). For Kohn, one of the worst illusions is that of 'national sovereign independence', the belief that a nation could be based on the 'non-intervention of the "foreigner" in "our" affairs'. Freud had famously argued in *Moses the Man*, his last major work, that the founder of the Jewish people had been an Egyptian. Edward Said's recent analysis of Freud's text as offering to the modern world the idea of a nation created by a foreigner, would then place Freud in this early Zionist lineage of critique.[18] The vision of an isolated nationhood, Kohn writes, is an aberration, a 'ghostly phantom' ('Nationalism', p27). We can gauge just how radical this is by comparing it with Leon Pinsker, for whom it is the Jews without a homeland who are the 'ghosts', 'the dead walking among the living': 'We wish to be a nation like the others'.[19] For Kohn, the far greater danger comes from a nation, cut off from the world around it, trying to wrap itself anxiously, defensively, around its own core: 'we will not be able to do without the bayonets'. In 1948, the army of the new state united the Haganah, which drew its troops from the Zionist movements devoted to pioneering and communal living, and the Irgun, the paramilitary organisation that aspired to Jewish control over all of Transjordan and Palestine. Buber was aghast: 'The Israeli army, elements that are [physically and spiritually] rooted in the land and those that are not, mingle with each other', wrote Buber, '*stand up as a wall, conquer, vanquish*' (*Land of Two Peoples*, p250, my emphasis).

From the beginning, writes Hannah Arendt in her 1944 essay 'Zionism Reconsidered', Zionism wanted, more than anything, 'utopian national independence' (p156). But nations are not independent. To be a law (race, faith) unto yourself is a myth. Dramatically, Israel has offered the spectacle of that illusion - the belief and its necessary failure - playing itself out on the world's stage. Not for the first time, there is something fundamental about nationhood that Zionism, so determined and yet fumbling in the dark, *allows us to see*. 'He did not realise,' Arendt writes of Herzl, 'that the country he

17. Judah Leon Magnes, 'Like All the Nations?' [1930], in *A Land of Two Peoples*, p 447.
18. Edward Said, *Freud and the Non-European*, Verso and the Freud Museum, 2003.
19. Leon Pinsker, 'Auto-Emancipation!', in Hertzberg, p184, p194.

dreamt of did not exist, that there was no place on earth where a people could live like the organic national body that he had in mind and that the real historical development of a nation does not take place inside the closed walls of a biological entity' (p172).

'Paradoxical as it may sound', she argues, 'it was precisely because of this nationalist misconception of the inherent independence of a nation that the Zionists ended up making the Jewish national independence entirely dependent on the material interests of another nation' (p156). If nationalism is 'bad enough' when it trusts in 'nothing but the rude force of the nation', a nationalism dependent on the force of a foreign nation is 'certainly worse' (pp132-3). Arendt warns: 'the anti-Semitism of tomorrow will assert that Jews not only profiteered from the presence of the foreign big powers in that region but actually plotted and hence are guilty of the consequences' (p133). 'Only folly', she concludes, 'could dictate a policy which trusts a distant imperial power for protection, while alienating the good will of neighbours' (p162). Israel, as Arendt also predicted, would become utterly reliant on America. 'We feel our battle is with America', Ramallah politician Ramadan Safi told me in an interview in 2002, 'the tanks are American, the guns are American, the fighters are American'.

I t is one of the defining problems of Zionism that it imported into the Middle East a central European concept of nationhood that was already in the throes of decline. This was a concept of organic nationhood, founded on ethnicity and blood (or 'land, descent and the dead'). For Moses Hess, Ancient Judaism had in fact been the first such group in human history - romantic nationalism was therefore at once the legacy and destiny of the Jewish people. It was of course a myth, and as the century unfolded, the Jews, above all other people, would be its victim. Writing seventy years after the publication of *der Judenstaat*, historian J. Tauber of the Hebrew University of Jerusalem commented: 'Little did Hess, Mazzini, Mickiewicz and their like know that in endowing nationalism with the dimension of a Salvationist religion, and in transferring to it so much of the Socialist appeal, they were unwittingly offering a rationale to that type of racial, exclusive nationalism, which Hess so abhorred among the Germans, and indeed to anti-Semitism, in both its racial and social versions'.[20] Israel inscribes at its heart the very version of nationhood from which

---

20. J.L. Talmon, *Israel Among the Nations*, pp102-103.

the Jewish people had had to flee.

Furthermore, at the very moment when Israel was created to secure the future of the Jewish people, this version of statehood revealed not only its inherent dangers, but its radical inability to defend the very principles on which it had once been built. Like Kohn, Arendt traces the beginning of this failure, which reaches its climax for the Jews in the Second World War, to the catastrophe of the First: 'As for nationalism', she continues, 'it never was more evil nor more fiercely defended than since it became apparent that this once great and revolutionary principle of the national organisation of peoples could no longer either guaranteee true sovereignty of the people within, or establish a just relationship among different peoples beyond, the national borders' (*Zionism reconsidered*, p141). This is nationalism, in the words of Tom Nairn, trapped in 'the essentialist cage of regimented identity, flag-worship and armour-plated community' (*London Review of Books*, 24.6.04). National faith of this kind becomes belligerent and expansive because it is so vulnerable and so raw, defending boundaries of the body and mind that do not exist. For that very reason, it 'permits and excuses anything' (the words of Hans Kohn in 'Nationalism', p30, who could just as well be describing the politics of the pre-emptive war on terror today).

Picking up her pen, like Buber, in May 1948, Arendt predicts with uncanny prescience the future of the new nation after its victory in the coming war:

> The 'victorious' Jews would live surrounded by an entirely hostile Arab population, secluded inside ever-threatened borders, absorbed with physical self-defence to a degree that would submerge all other interests and activities. The growth of a Jewish culture would cease to be the concern of the whole people, social experiments would have to be discarded as impractical luxuries; political thought would centre around military strategy; economic development would be determined exclusively by the need of war.[21]

The nation cannot secure its own future. Surely, it is often asked, Jewish nationalism is justified by the need of the Jewish people to have a place in the world where they can feel safe? Or physically and mentally at ease - a place

---

21. 'To Save the Jewish Homeland - There is Still Time', May 1948, *The Jew as Pariah*, p187.

where, as Gordon wrote to Ahad Ha'am in 1912, the Jew does not have endlessly to check the beat of his national pulse. But the Jews are not safe in Israel today. Nor indeed at ease with themselves. Exactly as Arendt predicted, the ethos of survival 'at any price' has become brutalised, and now, after 38 years in the occupied territories, is placing not just the safety but the sanity of the nation at risk. 'I was carried away by the possibility of acting in the most primal and impulsive manner,' Staff Sergeant Liran Ron Furer says of his experience in Gaza in his book *Checkpoint Syndrome*. 'Over time the behaviour […] became normative […] without fear of punishment and without oversight […] a place to test our personal limits - how tough, how callous, how crazy we could be' (quoted in *Ha'aretz*, 21.11.03).

'The question that looms', writes Ze'ev Schiff in *Ha'aretz* after the assassination of Hamas leader Sheikh Yassin in March 2004, 'is whether Israel has been attacked by the virus of a crazy state' (26.3.03). According to Amir Rappaport, writing in the newspaper *Ma'ariv*, Israel's air strikes on Gaza, which came in response to eight Qassam rockets fired by the Palestinians in October 2003, were deliberately disproportionate, to convey the message to the Palestinians that 'Israel has gone mad' (quoted in *Guardian*, 22.10.03). 'I see terrible graffiti - racist and Kahanist - that we accept offhandedly', writes Avraham Burg, former speaker of the Knesset and member of the Labour Party: the settlers and the right wing have left no 'place that is not affected by the nationalist consciousness' (*Ha'aretz*, 14.11.03).

In their different ways, in the dialogic space that runs between Buber, Arendt and Kohn, I hear all of them arguing that Zionism might have created a form of nationhood that would slash away politics, face its own dark beast, make room for the foreigner in its midst (or even more radically, perhaps, see itself as the stranger for the Arabs in Palestine). For a brief moment, Zionism had the chance of moulding a nation that would not be an 'expanded ego', but something else. At the opening of his essay 'Nationalism', Kohn describes how 'shifts of consciousness' are always accompanied by 'deep shocks', creating a time of 'disquiet, tension, isolation, dissociation'; such processes are 'obscure', 'ambivalent', 'uncertain' (p20). He could be describing glimpses of the unconscious, those moments - dreams, slips, symptoms - when the unconscious is allowed to slip past the wires, past the defences of the conscious mind, and makes its presence felt. Precisely because of the tragic peculiarity of Jewish history, because Jews have indeed in some sense been lost to the world - we do not have to reject Pinsker's 'ghosts' - Zionism, as a unique national movement, had the opportunity to forge a model of nationhood, neither belligerently nor pre-emptively, but ambivalent, uncertain, obscure, something closer to this disquieting and transformative space. But did not take it.

I n March 2004, Rabbis for Human Rights took out a full page advertisement in *Ha'aretz* to express their support for their colleague Rabbi Arik Ascherman, on trial in Jerusalem for trying to prevent the demolition of Palestinian homes. Returning to the vision I have tried to evoke here, they make their appeal to an earlier, lost, image of Zion: 'Zion will only be redeemed through justice and those who can return to her through acts of righteousness' (*Ha'aretz* 19.3.04).

In his book *Out of the Ashes - the Search for Jewish Identity in the Twenty-First Century*, Marc Ellis suggests that Jews often do not know that there was this history of dissent which has been 'forgotten or deliberately buried'.[22] Most simply, I have wanted to revive it. To show that Zionism was not one thing, that it knew itself better than it thinks. Reading these writers alongside the dominant voices of Israeli statehood is to be confronted with something like a split between lethal identification and grievous disenchantment; as if the state of Israel were offering its citizens and the rest of the world only the options of idealisation or radical dissent. It is also to be struck with an overwhelming sense of a moment missed, of voices silenced, of an argument, at terrible cost, re-repressed. Today we are all still suffering the loss of their critical, insightful, vision.

This is an edited extract from Jacqueline Rose's recent book, The Question of Zion, *Princeton University Press 2005.*

22. Marc H. Ellis, *Israel and Palestine Out of the Ashes - The Search for Jewish Identity in the Twenty-First Century*, Pluto 2002, pp35, 138.